Florian M

Assessment of
Data Integrity Risks
in Public Blockchain Systems

Bibliografische Information der Deutschen Nationalbibliothek:

Die Deutsche Nationalbibliothek verzeichnet diese Publikation in der Deutschen Nationalbibliografie; detaillierte bibliografische Daten sind im Internet über http://dnb.d-nb.de abrufbar.

Impressum:

Copyright © Studylab 2019

Ein Imprint der Open Publishing GmbH, München

Druck und Bindung: Books on Demand GmbH, Norderstedt, Germany

Coverbild: Open Publishing GmbH | Freepik.com | Flaticon.com | ei8htz

Assessment of Data Integrity Risks in Public Blockchain Systems

Since its first use in 2008, blockchain technology has come a long way and developed its functions from a simple distributed ledger to distributed virtual machines that execute smart contracts and much more. Blockchains have a potential application in many industries and offer great innovation potential for organizations. With all the opportunities and value new technologies can deliver, the risks are often neglected. In this paper risks to data integrity on blockchains are identified. Further the differences regarding data integrity among private and public blockchains are assessed. For the risk identification and the comparison between public and private systems a qualitative method with focus interviews is used, while the risk assessment is done with a quantitate online survey. The identified risks will be evaluated among their likelihood of occurrence and their possible consequences on the integrity of the data. Overall 11 risks have been identified which are applicable to public blockchains. Even though some of them got rated as a "High Risk" there is currently no evidence that a blockchain should be considered insecure. The identified risks should be taken into consideration before a public blockchain is implemented. The differences between public and private blockchains regarding data integrity are not rated, hence based on the collected data it cannot be generalized which design is more secure. The research results facilitate the decision between public and private systems. Based on the collected data and the literature review, the author discusses some actions that can be taken to mitigate the identified risks.

Acknowledgements

At this point I would like to thank all the people who accompanied and supported me during my master thesis. Special thanks to my family, without whose support my thesis would not have been possible. I would like to thank all interview partners and survey participants for their trust and support throughout the research process. A special thank you goes to the advisors at the Management Center Innsbruck and the University of Nebraska at Omaha which supported me the entire time.

Further I want to thank my fellow master students and the special people I meet and made friends with throughout the study program.

Table of Content

List of Figures

List of Tables

List of Abbreviations

BFT	Byzantine Fault Tolerance
CDN	Content Delivery Network
DApps	Distributed Applications
DDoS	Denial-of-Service
DLT	Distributed Ledger Technology
DPoS	Delegated Proof-of-Stake
DSA	Digital Signature Algorithm
ECDSA	Elliptic Curve Digital Signature Algorithm
ISACA	Information Systems Audit and Control Association
NIST	National Institute of Standards and Technology (U.S.)
P2P	Peer-2-Peer
PBFT	Practical Fault Tolerance
PKI	Public Key Infrastructure
PoS	Proof-of-Stake
PoW	Proof-of-Work
RACE	Research and Development in Advanced Communications Technologies in Europe
RIPEMD	RACE Integrity Primitives Evaluation Message Digest
RSA	Rivest–Shamir–Adleman (Algorithm)
SHA	Secure Hash Algorithms
SMR	State Machine Replication
SPOF	Single Point of Failure
SSOT	Single Source of Truth
TSS	Time-stamping service
U.S.C.	United States Code
UTXO	Unspent Transaction Output

X

1 Introduction

The term blockchain has become one of the main IT related buzzwords in the industry. Random organizations used the term blockchain in their company name to
increase their share value. An article by Easton(2018)shows that an iced tea-maker
was able to boost its share price temporary by 180% by changing the business
name to "Long Blockchain Corp.". Blockchain found its first real-world utilization
with the cryptocurrency Bitcoin, which was developed by the pseudonym Satoshi
Nakamoto in 2008 and launched in 2009. Since Bitcoins launch, more than 1500
other cryptocurrencies are currently on the market, which mostly also utilize
blockchain technology (CoinMarketCap, 2018). Almost every industry tries to get
in touch with blockchain to leverage their business. The "Gartner Hype Cycle for
Emerging Technologies", which is a depiction that shows maturity and adoption of
trending technologies, shows, in its most recent issue that is available, that blockchain technology is currently in the phase called "Peak of Inflated Expectations".

With all this hype, the questions arise whether it is justified or blockchain technology will disappear again soon. A general answer to the success of blockchain is almost impossible, but from a technical perspective, the advantages that blockchain
could give are undisputable, especially when it comes to the basics of data security,
which are also known as the CIA (Confidentially, Integrity, Availability) triad.

When there is a big hype about a new technology there is always a gold-rush mood
where a lot of new people join and expect the greatest things. In this case, often
disadvantages or risks are forgotten or simply ignored.

1.1 Research Gap and Research Question

By implementing a not very mature technology, organizations have to be aware of
the disadvantages of the technology. There is some literature published about security problems within blockchain technology. Karame and Androulaki(2016)
studied the security of blockchain, especially of Bitcoin. Bitcoin is using a public
and permission less blockchain, where every participant in the network can change
the ledger stored on the blockchain (Nakamoto, 2008). A lot of researcher addresses the advantages that blockchain can bring to industries and organizations,
but the conducted literature review of the author showed, that there are currently
no publications that address the threats that blockchain can bring to data integ-
rity.As described by Boritz(2005) data integrity is an essential part to data quality
and should therefore have a high priority in any information system. While there is

already a lot of discussions going on how blockchain can achieve data integrity there is currently no publication that addresses the risks, that the implementation of a blockchain can bring to data integrity. To narrow down the research this thesis focuses only on the public type blockchains, although a short comparison of the risks is done to be able to deliver more complete research results. While the differences are often discussed for example by Antonopoulos(2015) or Bashir(2018) they are not compared on a data integrity level. To enhance the contribution to the current state of research the identified risks are rated among their likelihood and the impact on data integrity.

This results in the following research questions:

RQ1: WHAT ARE RISKS WITHIN PUBLIC BLOCKCHAIN SYSTEMS REGARDING DATA INTEGRITY?

RQ2: WHAT ARE THE DIFFERENCES FOR DATA INTEGRITY WITHIN PUBLIC AND PRIVATE BLOCKCHAINS?

RQ3: WHAT ARE THE LIKELIHOOD AND CONSEQUENCES FOR EACH IDENTFIED RISK?

1.2 Motivation

Blockchain is one of the hot trending topics in the IT industry now. Such innovative technologies offer always a great opportunity to do research on. The author is also interested in blockchain technology and got already in contact with it by using cryptocurrencies. Blockchain and cryptocurrencies (especially Bitcoin) have proven their right of existence, when observing the constant increasing adaption and awareness by consumers and organizations (Thompson, 2018). Big tech companies like IBM or Microsoft offer blockchain services in their cloud environments or even contribute to the development of open sources blockchains. Also, as a future employee within the IT and consulting industry it is necessary to have knowledge about new and innovative technologies all the time, especially when the technology has the potential to disrupt whole industries. Furthermore, the author is convinced that the conducted research will deliver a significant value to organizations that consider implementing blockchain technologies in any way.

1.3 Value Proposition

The aim of this research is to contribute to the current state of research on block-chain technology and to support organizations when considering the implementation of a blockchain in their IT infrastructure.

Value is delivered for organizations by identifying risks, that the organization may have not been aware of. The evaluation of the identified risks can be seen by organizations as basis where they can add or remove risks depending on the system and design the organization intends to use.

From an academic perspective research about blockchain technology can be done in various fields of study. According to Risius and Spohrer(2017) most of the publications are in the field of computer science and information system, but there are also publications involving blockchain in finance, political science or law. Risius and Spohrer(2017) proposed a research framework which works as a guideline on which topics regarding blockchain research should be conducted. In this framework various levels of analysis are defined which are "Users & Society", "Intermediaries", "Platforms" and "Firms and Industries". These various levels can overlap in a research project, but their primary focus is to inspire future research. Beside the level of analysis, the framework defines different activities which are "Design & Features", "Measurement and Value" and "Management and Organization". The research of this thesis on conducted of the level "Platforms" and assesses "Design & Features". By following the blockchain research framework provided by Risius and Spohrer(2017), the academic relevance is ensured.

1.4 Outline

The background section of this master thesis will introduce the reader to the basic literature of blockchain technology and data security, especially data integrity and IT risk management. At the end of this section the reader should be able to understand what a blockchain is and how it works and what data integrity is and why it is an essential part of data / information security. Chapter 3 explains the research methodology for the risk identification, while the following Chapter presents the first empirical results. Next the results of the risk identification are briefly discussed and explained. In Chapter 6 the research methiodal for the risk evaluation is described. While the subsequent Chapters discuss the results and the implications of the found results. Chapter 9 delineates the limitations and assumptions that apply to the conducted research. In the last Chapter a conclusion of the thesis is stated. The raw data of the research is not included in the appendix, but instructions how to reproduce the conducted research.

2 Background

This Chapter provides background information on the topics decentralized systems, blockchain technology & design, data security and IT risk management. The goal of this Chapter is to provide the knowledge needed for the conducted research.

2.1 Centralized, Decentralized& Distributed Systems

Blockchains are distributed and decentralized system, hence it is important to understand the properties and parameters of these system designs.

At the beginning of the computer era, systems were big in size and expensive in acquisition and maintenance. These systems processed 1 instruction per second where nowadays systems can execute millions of instructions per second. All of processing was done in a single unit, which is called a centralized system (Tanenbaum & van Steen, 2016). The centralized architecture is still used by mainframes, even though mainframes are also able to operate in a cluster and can therefore be a distributed computing system (Weller, 2007).

In literature there is no single definition of the term distributed system. According to Tanenbaum and van Steen(2016) a distributed system is defined as:

> "[...] a collection of independent computers that appear to the user of the system as a single computer."

Andrews(2000) states that a distributed system consists of numerous computing systems that have their own random access memory (RAM). As there is no general definition of a distributed system the author will stick to the definition by Tanenbaum and van Steen(2016) for this thesis.

According to Grosch(1953) the power of a computer increase in proportion to the square of its cost. While this has been true for the mainframe era, it is not anymore nowadays because of the usage of microprocessors in computers. More computers (also called nodes) with less computing power are cheaper than one single system with the same processing power. This gives distributed systems an economical advantage against centralized systems. Distributed systems can achieve a higher overall performance, which would be not achievable by using just a single, centralized processing unit, simply due to physical limitations. By utilizing more than one processing unit, distributed systems omit a single point of failure (SPOF) and increases the reliability of the system by adding more nodes. When using or implementing distributed systems there are also some drawbacks. Distributed systems need a reliable network and have problems with security when it comes to data access. Systems that are distributed need specialized software to be able to deliver the advantages described (Tanenbaum & van Steen, 2016).

A very common perspective on distributed and decentralized systems was published by Baran(1964). Baran says decentralized systems use a hierarchy, while distributed systems are organized in a mesh and centralized systems are an organized in a solitary star. The publication of Baran is focused on communication networks and shown in Figure 1.

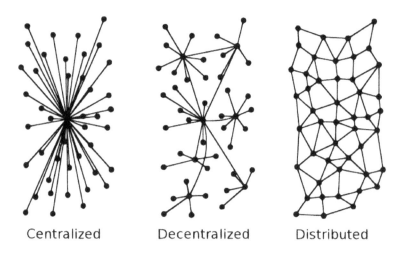

Centralized   Decentralized   Distributed

Figure 1: Architecture styles
(Baran, 1964, p. 2)

The Ethereum co-founder, blockchain expert and researcher Buterin(2017) provides a perspective on decentralized architecture that is more in-depth According to him decentralization in a system can be achieved on different levels. While centralization and distribution focus on the physical architecture of a system, decentralization can be achieved on an architectural, political and logical layer. A system that is decentralized on an architectural level is like a distributed system, where a number of individual nodes are interconnected. Political decentralization describes the control of a system. If a system is controlled by a single entity it is seen as centralized otherwise decentralized. The third level, logical decentralization, focuses on the data structure of the system. A system with one monolithic data object is logically centralized where amorphous systems do not share the data and are therefore logically decentralized.

In Table 1 some technologies are listed that achieve a certain level of decentralization. A content delivery network (CDN) is architecturally decentralized, by using webservers across the globe. These servers are controlled by one company, which makes the CDN politically centralized. Logical decentralization can also be seen in this case as the separation of databases. CDN often use different database on each web server, therefore it has a decentralized logic. The BitTorrent networks offers decentralization on all 3 levels. Compared to the CDN BitTorrent is not regulated or controlled by a single entity, therefore it also has decentralized politics. The third example, blockchain systems, offer decentralization in architecture and political. A blockchain behaves like a single computer and has a commonly agreed state, which results in a centralized logic.

	Content Delivery Network (CDN)	BitTorrent	Blockchain systems (e.g. Bitcoin)
Decentralized Architecture	X	X	X
Decentralized Politic		X	X
Decentralized Logic	X	X	

Table 1: Examples of Decentralized Systems
based on Buterin (2017)

By sticking to the approaches of (Tanenbaum & van Steen, 2016) and Buterin (2017) in conclusion can be said, distributed system offers an architecture, where the processing power is distributed among several nodes, which brings advantages in scalability, economy and overall performance. The decentralization of politics (control) enables a system to work independent from organizations and governments on its own. Logical decentralization exists when the system appears to be a single system. According to the definition by Tanenbaum and van Steen(2016), provided earlier, a distributed system is never fully decentralized because it appears as a single system to the user.

2.2 Blockchain Technology

After discussing the properties of decentralized and distributed systems in Chapter 2.1, this section explains the properties and parameters of blockchains systems. This includes the origin, components and design of a blockchain system.

There is no common definition in literature for a blockchain, most of them refer to the cryptocurrency Bitcoin. Bitcoin is a decentralized and trustless cash system which transactions are stored on a public ledger called blockchain (Swan, 2015). From a technical perspective a blockchain is a network of public databases, which keep in the case of bitcoin, track of all conducted transactions.

This Chapter uses the example of the bitcoin blockchain, to show exemplary architecture & protocol design, simply because it is the most established and developed blockchain and has therefore proven the validity of the used concepts.

2.2.1 Genesis

The basics principles of a blockchain are not new within the IT industry. A major influence of blockchain technology had the publication of Haber and Stornetta(1991). Proposed as "a naive solution" Haber and Stornetta(1991) described a time-stamping solution, where all clients send their documents to a trusted time-stamping service (TSS) which time stamps them and keeps them in record. This design raised several questions about privacy, bandwidth, storage and trust, which makes it not useable. To tackle those problems the utilization of cryptographic hashes was proposed, where only the hashes are transmitted to the TSS instead of the document itself. Another addition was the use of digital signatures. After the TSS received a hash, the TSS digitally signs it and sends the new signed hash (certificate) back to the client, which makes storing the data irrelevant for the TSS. With this design the TSS could still issue void timestamps, therefore Haber and Stornetta implemented a linking function between the issued hashes. This makes it for the TSS impossible to issue wrong timestamps. The TSS cannot issue a future time stamp, because the issued certificate must contain bits from immediately preceded requests.

This proposed design by Haber and Stornetta(1991) was an immutable chain of document certificates consisting of document hashes, time stamps and signatures of participating parties. This was a big step to the current state of art in blockchain designs, but Bayer, Haber, and Stornetta(1993) added another essential feature, the Merkle tree. The previous proposed solution was vulnerable to a flood of banal transactions, so Bayer et al.(1993) published a solution where many unnoteworthy events are merged into one big event. This is done by hashing 2 documents in one single hash and publish this hash, this procedure is called a hash- or Merkle tree. Another important step for the development of the blockchain were publication by Dwork and Naor(1993) and Back(2002) where a principle called hashcash was presented. Hashcash was initially designed to avoid spam emails and denial-of-service attacks (DDoS), by forcing the user (for example the sender of an email) to use a moderate amount of computing power to generate a hash, which is included in the email header. This hash needs to fulfill requirements (e.g. start with a zero) and can be only found via trial-and-error. The process of finding a hash via trial-and-error is called proof-of-work (PoW).

By adopting the previous described technical principles, Nakamoto(2008) published the first design of a blockchain, the bitcoin blockchain. The intend of bitcoin is to send and receive digital coins by using digital signatures and hashing algorithms. While bitcoin was proposed in 2008 the first block also called genesis block was mined on 3 January 2009[1]. Bitcoin is designed as an electronic peer-to-peer cash system on the top of the internet (Nakamoto, 2008). In a peer-to-peer (P2P) network, participants are equal and are connected in a mesh to each other. When referring back to Chapter 2.1, a P2P network is a distributed on an architectural level, with no central server (Tanenbaum & van Steen, 2016). The bitcoin network is a collection of nodes operating in a P2P network and using the bitcoin protocol for communication.

2.2.2 Components in a Blockchain System

A blockchain has several components in its system, which can be physical or digital. This Chapter explains the main components / terms of the bitcoin blockchain.

Digital Signatures

According to the National Institute of Standards and Technology(2013), a digital signature is a mechanism to verify the origin, authentication and integrity of electronic data. A digital signature can also be used to detect whether the data has been changed after signing or not. Each signature is a pair of keys which includes a private and a public key. To sign a document the private key of the key pair is

---

[1] This data can be seen with any kind of bitcoin block explorer, for example:
https://blockchain.info/block-in-
dex/14849/000000000019d6689c085ae165831e934ff763ae46a2a6c172b3f1b60a8ce26f

necessary, therefore it should stay secret and be only available to the owner of the keypair. A digital signature cannot be forged by simple copying from a previous signed document. To validate a digital signature, the public key is used, therefore there is no need to keep this key secret, because it is not possible to sign any documents with it. To obtain a key pair most of the time a digital signature algorithm (DSA) or elliptic curve digital signature algorithm (ECDSA) is used, but in some cases also a Rivest–Shamir–Adleman (RSA) algorithm. By using these mathematical algorithms, it is currently not possible to derive the private key of the public key. Digital signatures can also include domain parameters, for example if a digital signature is created to replace analog signatures, this may be the name of the person or the organization the individual is working for. All domain parameters within digital signatures are public (National Institute of Standards and Technology, 2013).

Address

Bitcoin is designed as a payment solution and therefor needs and address to transfer the digital coins to. To generate a bitcoin address, first a public/private key pair is created utilizing ECDSA. The address is not the public key itself, but is derived from it, by using several steps which include the hash functions SHA-256 and RIPEMD-160 and the Base58Check encoding scheme (Christin & Safavi-Naini, 2014). In the bitcoin environment an address is a unique string from 26 up to 35 characters, that is used by transactions to allocate origin and destination. An example of a bitcoin address is 1A1zP1eP5QGefi2DMPTfTL5SLmv7DivfNa, which was the first address ever used for receiving bitcoin[2]. The balance related to an address is public available on the blockchain and can be retrieved by looking up an address in a blockchain explorer. The smallest amount of bitcoin possible is 1 Satoschi, which equals 10^{-8} Bitcoin. It is also possible to create an address, that is shared within 2 or more parties. To be able to execute a transaction from such an address a defined number of signatures from the parties is required. For example, if 3 people share an address they can define that at least 2 people out of the 3 need to sign with their private key to make a transaction. This type of address is called multi-signature (or Multisig) address. Transactions are signed with the 256-bit private key number (Karame & Androulaki, 2016). A new bitcoin address can be generated offline, to avoid that a third party gets access to the private key. Therefore it is

---

[2] https://block-
chain.info/en/tx/4a5e1e4baab89f3a32518a88c31bc87f618f76673e2cc77ab2127b7afdeda3
3b

theoretically possible that 2 individuals generate the same address, although it is highly unlikely because there are 2^{256} possibilities of potential private keys for bitcoin. (Antonopoulos, 2015). As explained earlier the address generation uses RIPEMED-160, which means there are only 2^{160} addresses available for 2^{256} private keys. Hence it is theoretically possible that the same address is derived from more than one private key.

Wallet

According to Franco(2015) a bitcoin wallet is a collection of one or more private keys. Compared to physical wallets, bitcoin wallets can be easily copied by duplicating the private key. As explained in the previous paragraph about addresses, it is possible to operate a distributed wallet by using a multi-signature address. When talking about a wallet people often mean the wallet software. A regular wallet holds banknotes and the owner of the wallet can check the amount by counting the notes. A bitcoin wallet works different, because the available amount of bitcoin is not stored. To see the balance of an address the wallet software queries the whole blockchain and collects all transactions with the provided address as origin or destination. The result of this query is called unspent transaction output (UTXO) and shows the delta between inputs and outputs to the address (Franco, 2015).

Block

The blockchain is a linked list of blocks that contain transaction data. Each block has a unique hash which it can be identified with. A blockchain block consists of a header, and transactional data. Within the bitcoin blockchain, the header includes information about the used software version, hash of the previous block, the Merkle root, timestamp, difficulty target and a nonce. Another way to identify a block is by its height. The height can also be seen as the number that the block has (Antonopoulos, 2015). The first block had height 0 and the last published block as of writing this thesis has the height 537017 and contains 2467 transactions[3]. Blocks are created by miners and then published to the network. More on mining in the next paragraph.

---

[3] See block #537017: https://www.block-chain.com/btc/block/00000000000000000002268d0e61dc6e4c7bbdb69696abfa8248503ae
c6508594

Mining

When a transaction is made it is published to the network. Nodes operating on this network collect and verify transactions by given rules, but do not confirm them yet. A transaction is unconfirmed when it has been not included in one of the blocks of the chain. The pool of unconfirmed transactions is called transaction pool or memory pool (Antonopoulos, 2015). To get a transaction confirmed it must be included in a block. A node that is participating in mining on the network, sets up a block includes transactions and tries to find the hash for the block using the SHA-256 algorithm. To create a valid block, the hash of the block header must start with a defined number of zeros. A higher number of starting zeros makes it more difficult for miners to find a valid block and is therefore referred as mining difficulty. When the block header is hashed with SHA-256 and the requirements of the hash are not meet, the miner changes the nonce in the header and creates a new hash. This is the implementation of the hashcash algorithm in bitcoin for proof-of-work. After finding a hash that meets the criteria the miner publishes the new block to the network. Every other network node verifies the validity of the block and adds it to the existing chain (Bashir, 2017).

Nodes

Not every node on the bitcoin network is operating as a miner. According to Antonopoulos(2015) there can be distinct types of nodes on a blockchain network, which are depicted in Table 2, where the first column defines the name of the node and the following columns describe the functions, the node is performing.

Name	Mining	Copy of full blockchain	Network routing	Wallet Software
Reference Client	x	x	x	x
Full Node		x	x	
Solo Miner	x	x	x	
Lightweight Wallet			x	x

Table 2: Types of nodes
adopted from Antonopoulos (2015)

The terms of mining and wallet software have already been covered in the previous paragraphs. A full copy of the blockchain means a node has stored the whole blockchain, not only the headers, on its local hard drive. This enables a node to validate transactions and blocks that are sent across the network. This is where the network routing functionality comes in. This function enables the node to participate in the P2P network, and to send / receive new transactions and blocks.

2.2.3 Bitcoin Blockchain Design

The bitcoin blockchain is a chain of blocks which contain financial transactions. Every block is linked to the previous block by including the hash of the previous block, which proves that a certain state was valid at the defined point of time, because the past cannot be changed without a very high investment in computing power. This is due to the parent / child relationship that blocks have. A block contains the hash of the previous block header, therefore if a block changes all subsequent would have to change too. Therefore a block gets more secure the more subsequent blocks exist (Antonopoulos, 2015). A valid hash for a block has to start with a defined number[4] of zero bits. To find the hash of the block POW is used. After successful finding a suitable hash, the miner is rewarded with a mining incentive, which depends on the block height. The bitcoin network is a collection of individual nodes, that operate in a distributed manner, and can be joined by anyone without any special permission, which is also called a permissionless public blockchain (more on that in Chapter 2.2.5).

Bitcoin increases the level of privacy for users by eliminating the trusted third party, normally used for validating financial transactions (Nakamoto, 2008). The simplified blockchain header in Figure 2 shows the inclusion of the Merkle root of all transactions. Within the bitcoin network, all transactions are at the bottom of the tree and hashed in pairs of 2, until only one (the Merkle root) hash remains. This procedure can work with an arbitrarily number of transactions and the Merkle root will always be 32 Byte. Figure 3 shows what a Merkle tree of bitcoin transactions looks like. Bitcoin uses the collision free hash algorithm SHA256 (Bashir, 2018).

---

[4] Within the bitcoin system this is a variable and is recalculated every 2016 blocks. This step is also known as difficulty adjustment.

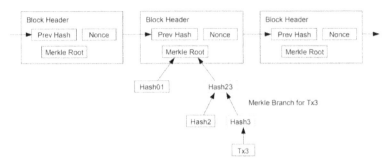

Figure 2: Simplified bitcoin block design
(Nakamoto, 2008)

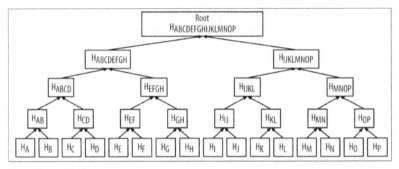

Figure 3: Merkle Tree
(Antonopoulos, 2015)

Blockchain is often referred to as a database, which is not correct, because the blockchain network doesn't have a database itself, but nodes that participate in the system have one. For example, Bitcoin Core, which is used to run a node on the bitcoin network, uses a LevelDB to store data of the bitcoin blockchain. The above described architecture (blocks that contain hashed transaction data and are linked to the previous block) is the basic blockchain architecture. Most blockchain system are based on this architecture and are then individualized by using a different protocol. The protocol contains specifications about the block size (e.g. bitcoin uses a maximum block size of 1MB at the moment), used hashing algorithm, etc. As mentioned the bitcoin blockchain is a public and permissionless system and therefore a consensus must be achieved within the network. In other financial systems this step is done centralized by a trusted bank automatically or manually. As there is no central authority, that can be trusted in the bitcoin network a decentralized consensus must be achieved. Every node running on the bitcoin network has a full copy of the bitcoin blockchain. If a new block is added to the chain every node can check its validity by simple rules that are defined. In bitcoin, this consensus is emergent because there is no voting or similar going on (Antonopoulos, 2015).

For the further reading it is important to understand that the blockchain itself is not a medium for data storage, rather than a distributed network of nodes that store data, which is in the case of bitcoin is financial transaction data. As conclusion of this Chapter can be said that the unique architectural characteristics of a blockchains are the decentralized consensus, the chain of blocks, where every block is linked to its parent block which makes the blockchain immutable. These properties differentiate blockchain systems from other systems, but within blockchain systems there is a wide variety of types possible. These distinct types will be covered in the following Chapter.

2.2.4 Categories of Blockchains

Blockchain differ in its functionality, depending on their state of evolution. Therefore, in literature blockchains are often classified in categories from blockchain 1.0 up to blockchain 3.0. The bitcoin blockchain, is a prime example for a 1.0 blockchain. Blockchains in this category aim to be a cryptocurrency and to solve problems regarding financial transactions. A blockchain of the second generation includes contract functionality. This enables a blockchain system to operate beyond simple financial transactions in a whole market. This could be stocks, mortgages, smart contracts or smart property. The most advanced blockchain category is 3.0. Blockchains in this category are not only used in financial markets, but rather in government, health, science and many more. (Swan, 2015).

Within this thesis this three-tier approach is used for categorizing blockchain systems. There are also opinions (e.g. Unibright.io) that state 4 different categories of blockchains, where 3.0 refers to decentralized applications (DApps) and blockchain 4.0 to the industry adoption. Swan(2015) sees DApps as part of blockchain 2.0 systems. In conclusion can be said, there is no clearly defined definition in literature for the different tiers of blockchain systems.

Blockchain systems with smart contracts and decentralized applications are covered more in depth within Chapter 2.2.6

2.2.5 Properties of Blockchains

Blockchains have unique properties in its system and protocol design which define their area of application. Within this Chapter the properties accessibility / visibility, tokenization, block design and consensus mechanism are discussed.

Accessibility / visibility

The bitcoin blockchain, is not owned by any company, central authority or the developer team. All potential users that are willing to can participate as a node in the bitcoin network and read / write to the blockchain hence bitcoin is a public blockchain accessible and visible for everyone. In contrast to public chains, private blockchains are only open to a selected group of individuals or organizations. Private blockchains are owned by a single entity and are not open to public, which makes them more appear like a cryptographical secured database (Bashir, 2018). Compared to traditional distributed databases a private blockchain offers the use of Smart Contracts (Lai & LEE Kuo Chuen, 2018). Compared to public blockchains, private ones are not trustless and often not fully decentralized. When talking about public and private blockchains often the words permissioned and permissionless are used as a synonym, which is misleading. A permissioned blockchain is a trade-off between the public and private design. In a permissioned blockchain system, a potential user must verify their identity before being able to participate. After the verification a user can take on different roles within the blockchain system (Bashir, 2018).

When refereeing back to the discussion about decentralization in Chapter 2.1 and in more detail to Table 1: Examples of distributed systems, based on Buterin (2017), public blockchains achieve more decentralization than private or permissioned systems, because public systems use decentralized politics. More decentralization does not mean all public chains are superior to private or permissioned ones, it depends on the area of application and the purpose the blockchain has to serve.

Tokenization

The intended purpose of the bitcoin blockchain, as stated by Nakamoto (2008), is to create a digital cash system with its own currency, hence bitcoin issued its own coin as a currency, which makes it a tokenized blockchain. In the context of blockchain, coins are a unit of a cryptocurrency, while tokens are a digital representation of an asset. These digital coins or tokens operate as an incentive layer on the blockchain, mostly as an incentive for mining. Therefore, tokenization is closely related to the consensus mechanism and the accessibility of a blockchain. Public chains use PoW or PoS to achieve consensus and distribute tokens or coins to the miner of the newest block. Private chains often do not rely on mining or staking as consensus algorithm and therefore don't have a token or coin issued, which is called token-less blockchain (Lai & LEE Kuo Chuen, 2018).

Block design

Bitcoin has currently blocks that are 1MB in size, created approximate every 10 minutes and contain financial transactions. The size and speed of blocks is specified in the source code of the bitcoin protocol and therefore it can be unique to every blockchain. The time between blocks in a PoW secured blockchain is not defined in a timeframe, rather than a difficulty for the PoW mechanism. This difficulty is determined dynamically and based on the total processing power on the network. An increase of mining power since the last difficulty calculation leads to a difficulty increase, while a reduction of mining power causes a reduction of mining difficulty. In the case of bitcoin, the difficulty adjustment is done every 2016 blocks, which equals approx. 14 days (Antonopoulos, 2015).

Compared to bitcoin, the Ethereum blockchain uses a different approach regarding block size and a slightly changed difficulty adjustment. On Ethereum the block size is not determined by the size of its content, but rather the amount of fees that occur. Fees for the execution of transactions or smart contracts on Ethereum are specified in gas. When a block reaches its gas limit (currently 8 million) the block is considered full. The gas limit is defined by the miners which can vote on increasing or decreasing the limit. Compared to bitcoin, the block time on Ethereum does have a targeted time range. When the previous block was mined in under 10 seconds the difficulty will increase, between 10 and 19 seconds the difficulty will stay the same, a block time of equal or greater than 20 seconds will decrease the mining difficulty. Ethereum uses a "Difficulty Bomb" which increases the mining difficulty at a certain point so much, that it is not profitable anymore. This method is used to force the switch from PoW to PoS consensus mechanism (Antonopoulos & Wood, 2018).

Consensus Mechanism

Blockchain solved the problem of decentralized consensus on a certain state. To achieve consensus across the network, different mechanisms can be used, as explained in Chapter 2.2.3, bitcoin uses PoW. To achieve consensus with the PoW mechanism, a lot of computational resources are required, which leads to high energy consumption. For PoW a variety of hashing algorithms can be implemented.

Another mechanism that is already used in blockchains for cryptocurrencies is Proof-of-Stake (PoS). This mechanism relies on market forces rather than computing power. The number of tokens owned by the participating node defines the chance to add a block to the existing chain. By owning more tokens in the network, the interest of the miner to secure the network and therefore his tokens increase. Another type of PoS is Delegated Proof-of-Stake (DPoS), where the users vote for witnesses which generate consensus (Lai & LEE Kuo Chuen, 2018). These described mechanisms are suitable for blockchains that use tokens or coins to incentive the miner (PoW) or the voter (PoS & DPoS) and as a protection against 51% attacks. In token-less blockchains different and often proprietary mechanisms that make use of classical state machine replications (SMR) to provide fault tolerance are used (Lai & LEE Kuo Chuen, 2018). A state machine replication can be seen as copies of a system (at least 3 to provide fault tolerance) which maintain the same state or output (Schneider, 1990). For example, Hyperledger Fabric utilizes state machines to achieve Byzantine fault tolerance (BFT) when ordering transaction, which results in one transaction list every participating node has agreed on, even if there were malicious nodes on the network. (Bashir, 2018)(Castro & Liskov, 2002).

Table 3 shows a summary of the used hash algorithms and consensus mechanism among the biggest cryptocurrencies by June 2018.

Rank[5]	Currency	Hash Algo-rithm	Consensus Mechanism	Reference / Comment
1	Bitcoin	SHA-256	PoW	Nakamoto(2008)
2	Ethereum	Ethash	PoW	Bashir(2018), Buterin(2014)
3	Ripple	ECDSA	Byzantine Consensus	Schwartz, Youngs, and Britto(2014)
4	Bitcoin Cash	SHA-256	PoW	Fork of Bitcoin
5	EOS	-	-	Currently an ERC-20 Token on the Ethereum Blockchain
6	Litecoin	Scrypt	PoW	Litecoin Foundation(2018)

---

[5] The cryptocurrencies are ranked regarding market capitalization, retrieved from
https://www.coinmarketcap.com on June 6 2018

7	Cardano	OUROBOROS	PoS	Kiayias, Russel, Bernardo, and Oliynykov(2017)
8	Stellar	Undefined	Byzantine Consensus / SCP	Mazieres(2016)
9	IOTA	Curl	PoW	IOTA Foundation(2018)(IOTA Foundation), Popov(2017)

Table 3: Used Consensus Mechanism and Hash Algorithms

2.2.6 Smart Contracts & Decentralized Applications

Contracts are a critical element in an economy, especially in finance. Bitcoin, as a single payment transaction system, is currently not able to process complex financial contracts[6]. While economic contracts consist of a mandatory payment for a service or good in an exchange, financial contracts are purely cash flow based. Financial contracts are mostly expressed in number and are therefore well suited for self-execution and smart contracts (Brammertz & Mendelowitz, 2018). The principles of smart contracts are not new, it origins from Szabo(1997). The most used smart contract platform based on blockchain is Ethereum. There are currently (May 2018) more than 26,364 contracts that have a verified source code [7]. A very common used standard for Ethereum smart contracts is the ERC20 token standard, which is used to issue and manage digital tokens based on the Ethereum blockchain. The specific code for every smart contract is public available and can be seen by using a blockchain explorer[8]. In the Ethereum whitepaper, published by Buterin(2014), the use cases of smart contracts are separated in full-financial, semi-financial and non-financial. As earlier discussed, Brammertz and Mendelowitz(2018) only sees application for cash-flow contracts, but Buterin(2014), planned to use Ethereum also for non-cash-flow contracts such as voting, decentralized governance and even cloud computing. The execution of a smart contract requires a fee which is issued to the miner, that executes the contract code (Buterin, 2014).

---

[6] Bitcoin can execute simple code with Bitcoin Script

[7] https://etherscan.io/contractsVerified

[8] Example EOS Token: https://etherscan.io/address/0x86fa049857e0209aa7d9e616f7eb3b3b78ecfdb0#code

As smart contracts, DApps are not specifically build to run on a blockchain, but most decentralized apps are a derivative of smart contracts. The BitTorrent peer-2-peer network is used for several DApps. For example, OpenBazaar is a decentralized selling platform. Centralized platforms for offering goods and services like eBay have policies and fees for using the platform. OpenBazaar works with the BitTorrent protocol and has therefore no central authority, and for decentralized payments bitcoin is used. To have a complete decentralized application the app has to satisfy four criteria's: No single point of failure (SPOF), internal currency (tokens), decentralized consensus and open source code (Raval, 2016). A recent example of a DApp running on the Ethereum blockchain is the game CryptoKitties[9], which is a game where users can collect and breed digital cats. For each different action that can be taken with one of those digital cats, a smart contract exists. The complete code for the application can be seen at the contract address 0x06012c8cf97bead5deae237070f9587f8e7a266d.

2.3 Data Security

This Chapter will introduce data security with an emphasis on data integrity, which is a main component of this thesis. Furthermore, the current situation of data integrity in blockchain systems will be discussed.

The amount of intangible assets within an organization is continually increasing.According to Vacca(2017), the amount of intangible assets reached an average of 84% within S&P 500 organizations, in 2015. To protect corporate value, it is necessary to have a data & information security plan in place. The National Institute of Standards and Technology(2018) defines a cybersecurity framework to help organizations to identify, assess, and manage cyber risks. According to the cybersecurity framework by NIST (2018) data security is achieved when:

> "Information and records (data) are managed consistent with the organization's risk strategy to protect the confidentiality, integrity, and availability of information."

The definition above is also known as the CIA (confidentiality, integrity and availability) triad. In the following, each of the three dimensions will be discussed in detail, whereby, particular emphasis will be put on integrity.

---

[9] Cryptokitties website: https://www.cryptokitties.co

The definition used by NIST, published in *44 U.S.C § 3542 Definitions*, describes confidentiality in the context of data security as:

"[...] preserving authorized restrictions on information access and disclosure, including means for protecting personal privacy and proprietary information."

Confidentiality can also be described as an inadvertent disclosure of data that has not been authorized. The availability of information and data is defined as timely and reliable access to it (44 U.S.C. § 3542 - DEFINITIONS).

Data Integrity

Integrity is a common term in data and information security, but there is no clear definition in literature. The it-governance association ISACA(2012) defines data integrity by the 3 attributes complete, accurate and valid. NIST however, defines integrity as a characteristic that prevents inappropriate changes and destruction to data and ensures authenticity and verifiability (Kissel, 2013). To establish a clear definition for data integrity,Boritz (2005) conducted a research study. Therein he created an integrity framework consisting of four core attributes and seven enablers. Those identified parameters have been rated regarding to importance and severity on a scale from 0 to10, where 0 is the lowest and 10 is the highest rate. As shown in Figure4 all attributes are rated regarding to importance and severity,whereby the attributes are not summarized into the four core attributes and seven critical success factors.

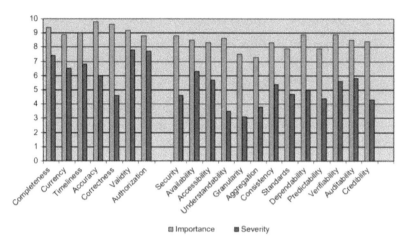

Figure 4: Importance and Severity of core attributes and enablers
(Boritz, 2005)

CoreAttributes

According to Boritz(2005), data integrity is often seen as representational faithfulness of data. An item has to fulfill at least the following described four core attributes to be considered as integer data.

The first core attribute is accuracy/correctness. The standard ISO 5725 published by the International Organization for Standardization(1994), defines accuracy as the closeness of a measurement to its true value. In the area of information technology and data management, data is perceived as accurate when the database reflects the data of the real world. Completeness, the second core attribute is related to accuracy because it is not possible to achieve 100% real-time completeness, due to limitations of existing information systems.Therefore a utterly accuracy is not possible (Boritz, 2005). Timeliness, the third core attribute of the framework, also called currency, refers to the degree to which data is current with the world it represents. The currency of data is in literature often described as the most important dimension of data quality (Loshin, 2011). The last and fourth core attribute is validity/authorization. Regarding to data security, validity means that stored informationrepresents real conditions and rules rather than properties of objects. For example, a transaction is valid, if it is approved by an authorized party (Boritz, 2005).

In summary it can be said that integer data has the following core attributes:

Accurate / Correct

Complete

Current / Timely

Validity / Authorization

Enablers

Compared to the core attributes, enablers are not characteristics of data integrity.They simply support to achieve data integrity even though none of the core attributes can be achieved completely in information systems.(They simply support and enable the achievement of the core attributes, even though none of the core attributes can be fully achieved in the information systems.)Boritz(2005) defines seven critical success factors for data integrity: Security, availability, understandability, consistency, dependability, verifiability and credibility.

For the research within this master thesis, the enablers are inferior to the core attributes, because the goal of this research is to determine threats to the core attributes rather than find out how to support the enablers to achieve integrity.
The goal of this research paper isto determine threats to the core attributes, rather than find out how to support the enablers to achieve integrity. Therefore, enablers are discussed inferior in this master thesis. Still the enablers can be used by the interview partners to identify possible threats to one or more core attributes.

2.4 IT Risk Management

Before getting started on managing risks related to IT it is important to understand what risk management in general is. According to Merna and Al-Thani(2008) risk management

> "[...] is a formal process that enables the identification, assessment, planning and management of risks."

For managing risks within an organization, there are several frameworks that support the process. The major framework in risk management is COSO ERM – Enterprise Risk Management Framework. As the name already states this framework works on an enterprise level which also includes IT related risks. Another approach for enterprise wide risk management is the family of ISO (International Organization of Standardization) 31000. Managing IT risks is a part of the IT governance and therefore it is also described in CoBIT5. CoBIT5 complies with enterprise level frameworks such as COSO but also covers IT security. In 2013, ISACA published the first version of CoBIT5 for Risk which helps to link IT risks to strategic enterprise objectives. As shown in Figure5 CoBIT for Risk can integrate other risk management standards such as COSO, ISO31000 and ISO27005.

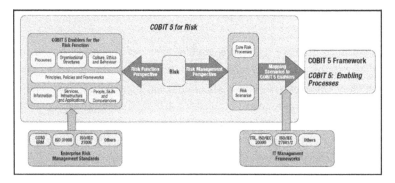

Figure 5: Scope of COBIT 5 for Risk

The standard ISO27005:2008 defines how to assess, treat and manage information security risks. In the following description of the process, the author will focus on the risk assessment only. The process for risk assessment is shown in Figure6.

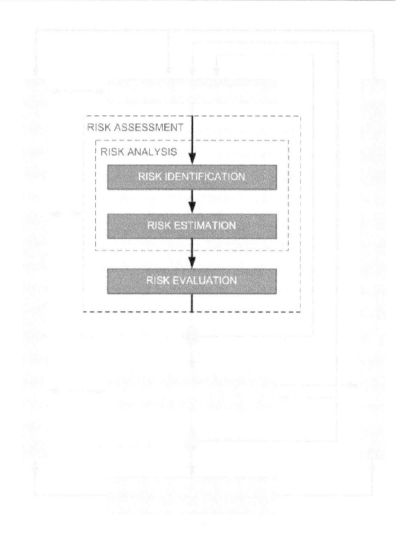

Figure 6: Risk Assessment Process
(ISO, 2011)

An assessment of risks consists of risk analysis and risk evaluation,while risk analysis is separated in risk identification and risk estimation. The goal of a risk identification is to identify the threat, the source where it comes from and the type of it (e.g. unauthorized action) (ISO, 2011). A source of a threat be every party that is interested in the system (ISO, 2013). Another part of the risk identification is to identify the vulnerabilities within the organization (e.g. Personnel, hardware, etc.)

and the consequences of it. Risk evaluation can be done qualitatively or quantitatively. The qualitative approach uses a scale of qualifying attributes (e.g. rare, possible and almost certain), while the quantitative estimation uses a scale with numerical values. Both methods evaluate the consequences and the likelihood of the identified risk. When matching the likelihood and consequences together, the level of risk can be determined. This leads to a list of risks with a value level assigned. Prioritizing the risks according to the previous determined value levels (quantitative or qualitative) concludes the step of risk evaluation (ISO, 2011).

2.5 Previous research

A lot of publications, blog posts and news articles discuss the advantages of blockchain technology, but the downsides and risks are way less discussed.

Antonopoulos(2015) discusses various consensus attacks specialized on bitcoin. At first the 51% attack. In this scenario, an attacker controls 51% or more mining power of within the blockchain network. This much mining power enables the attacker to execute denial-of-service (DDoS) attacks and double spend his own transactions. The 51% threshold of mining power almost guarantees the success, but it can also be successfulwith less than 51% of the mining power. Also, PoS blockchain systems are vulnerable to such an attack. To acquire 51% of the total supply of a cryptocurrency may sound expensive, but as described by Houy(2014), this can be achieved at almost no cost, if this happens in a very early stage of the blockchain lifespan.

Despite the previous described attack, there is also a threat of forks on public blockchain systems. Those can happen unwittingly when two miners find a new block and propagate it. This results in a fork until the following block for one of the previous two blocks is found (Antonopoulos, 2015, pp. 199–204).

Weber et al.(2017) discuss the availability in blockchain systems which is also one of the three major properties of data security. The currently and only academic publication that discusses data integrity in blockchain systems is Gaetani et al.(2017). This paper discusses how to achieve data integrity when a blockchain is used as a data management system, rather than integrity on the blockchain itself.

Li, Jiang, Chen, Luo, and Wen(2017) conducted a risk analysis of blockchain systems previously. This paper analyzed generic risks in blockchain without any limits. The identified risks are:

- 51% Vulnerability
- Private Key Security
- Criminal Activity
- Double Spending
- Transaction Privacy Leakage
- Criminal, vulnerable and under-optimized smart contracts
- Under-priced operations

The identified risks by Li et al.(2017) are generic risks and not focused on data integrity. Hence it cannot be ruled out that the research (results) conducted in this thesis will partly overlap with the results in the study by Li et al.(2017).Nevertheless, the results of the study by Li at al. (2017) will not be used as a basis for the research conducted in this thesis, due to the different focus of the study.

3 Qualitative Research Methodology

In this section the author will describe the research design that has been used to conduct the research. To answer the research question 1 and 2, it is necessary to gather and analyze data by utilizing a scientific method.

The first research objective of this master thesis is to find threats / risks to data integrity in public blockchain systems, or more loosely speaking, the problem of data integrity in blockchain systems. When problems must be identified and understood, explorative research is conducted. Explorative research deals mostly with qualitative data, which enables the researcher to better understand a concept or in this case a problem. The alternative to qualitative data is quantitative data, which determines the quantity or extend of a certain phenomenon in numbers.In contrast to quantitative methods like a survey, the purpose of qualitative research is not to make a generalization of a sample to a greater population (Zikmund, 2009).

The author has chosen to use a qualitative research approach to answer the first two research questions. To collect quantitative data about data integrity threats in blockchain data management systems, it would be necessary to get data of a high number of implementations within organizations. Due to the low adoption within organization it is not possible to gain credible quantitative data. To collect qualitative data, different methods can be used, which will be examined in the following Chapter.

3.1 Data Collection Method

After the decision to use qualitative data to answer the first two research questions, the next step is to define the method of data collection. Zikmund(2009) defines the following methods to collect data for explorative research: focus group interviews, depth interview and case studies. Beside Zikmund(2009) also other publications have suggestions for methods to collect qualitative data. For example Marschan-Piekkari(2004) adds ethnography as a method for gathering qualitative data. When it comes to data collection methods Liamputtong and Ezzy(2006) describe the same methods, with different wording, as the previous literature and in addition, memory-work, participatory action research.

Overall the author considered the following methods for collection qualitative data for the conducted research: In-depth interviews, focus group, case study, ethnography and memory-work.

In-depth interviews or also known as focus interviews, are semi- to unstructured and are conducted with one experienced interviewer and a single respondent at the time. This technique gives in depth understanding of the researched problem, and the point of view of the expert, which are often hard to find. Furthermore, interviews are also expensive to conduct and need precise analysis to merge the information from content, surface reactions and subconscious motivation. Compared to interviews, focus groups are unstructured and involve several participants at the same time. This gives the group the possibility to piggyback on each other ideas, but on the other hand this could lead the whole discussion in a single direction. Focus group interviews utilize a moderator and no interviewer. (Zikmund, 2009). Another possible method is to conduct a case study. A case study investigates on one or more individuals (e.g. organization, industry, group of people...) history, to answer a specific research question. Case studies can involve qualitative and quantitative data (Gillham, 2005). Ethnography is a method that is often found in anthropological research and is often referred to as community studies in sociology. Ethnography is often interpretative and focus on the culture of a specific cluster of groups. Memory work is a method that gathers data by study the past and its goal is liberation. This method is often seen in social research (Liamputtong & Ezzy, 2006).

After examining the applicability of all the considered methods, the author has chosen to conduct in-depth / focus interviews. At first ethnography and memory work is not a common research method in the field of information systems and are also not suitable to provide data that could answer the proposed research question. A case study is suitable for exploratory research by investigating one or more situations. To find threats to data integrity in blockchain data management systems, a case study would need the participation of one or more organizations in the research that had a situation of a data integrity incident in a blockchain data management system. Such events are handled with confidentially within organizations to prevent attacks from exploiting the security risk. Therefore, the author is not able to gain access to the data that would be needed to answer the research question.

3.2 Focus Interview

An interview is usually seen as a communication between two people (interviewer and respondent / interviewee). The reasons for conducting an interview are diverse, but when conducting it to solve a research problem it is called research interview. Interviews can be conducted structured, unstructured or semi structured.

Each of these three types enables the interviewer to be flexible within the interview, where structured interviews are the least flexible and unstructured interviews are the most flexible. Research interviews that are performed with an expert on the researched topic are never completely unstructured. In general, interviews can be designed to deliver breadth and depth, but especially in smaller research projects, a decision has to be made, which one to address. At the beginning of the interview the questions are much broader and with progress within the interview the interviewer narrows down the topic. By starting out with generic questions a collective understanding of wording and principles within the researched domain can be assured (Gillham, 2001). During an interview not only spoken words are produced, also non-verbal behavior and gestures are part of the data and have to be collected. This data is also included in the transcribed version of the interview (Miles, Huberman, & Saldaña, 2014).

To provide flexibility within the interviews, the author has chosen a semi-structured approach. Therefore, the author uses a set of predefined guiding questions that are used within the interview. This approach allows the author also to collect additional data, by digging deeper in the answers of the respondent.

3.2.1 Guiding Questions

Before the research interview personal data is collected. This includes the name, residency and job description, but is not included in the transcribe, to ensure full privacy to every respondent, further details on this in Chapter 3.1.3. When conducting a semi-structured interview, some predefined guiding questions are necessary. According to Gillham(2001) an interview starts with a very broad topic and then narrows the topic and questions down. By following this scheme, the author developed the following interview approach, which is depicted in Table 4.

Topic	Focus	Example Question
Integrity threats on Blockchain systems	Accuracy	In which situations a public blockchain may deliver inaccurate or wrong data?
	Completeness	How can data on a public blockchain be incomplete?
	Currency / Timeliness	Under what circumstances a public blockchain would deliver outdated information?
	Validity / Authorization	How can data stored in a public blockchain be invalid or not authorized?
Public and private chains	Security Differences	Do you see any difference regarding data security / integrity between public and private blockchains?

Table 4: Interview Guiding Questions

These questions will be asked in every conducted interview. Depending on the responses more questions are added to get more data about the ideas or concept the respondent is describing.

3.2.2 Selection of respondents

Interview partners are recruited by using the network of the author and the advisors of this thesis. Furthermore, after conducting the interview successful snowball sampling is used to find more appropriate candidates. To maintain the scope of the master thesis, but still be able to get the best possible results, a number of 10 to 15 interviews are conducted. The exact number is depending on the collected data and availability of appropriate interview candidates.

All names of the interviewees are anonymized by using a key table. The author randomly assigns a number to every conducted interview which are linked to name of the respondent. This linking table is exclusively accessible and available to the author of the thesis. The data includes a generic job title (e.g. blockchain developer, consultant...) and the geographical area of residence. To increase the privacy of respondents, this data will be abstracted, so no inference can be drawn to single individuals.

3.3 Ontology& Epistemology

After defining which and how to collect the data for the defined research the next step is to analyze the data. Qualitative data is collected as words and therefore not suitable for statistical analysis, like quantitative data. Therefore, qualitative data has to be interpreted and coded according to identified themes (Miles et al., 2014).

To analyze an interview, general assumptions according the research philosophy must be made, these are described in the following Chapter.

According to Hudson and Ozanne(1988), ontology can be defined as the nature of reality and social beings. Epistemology describes the relationship between the researcher and the reality (Perry, Riege, & Brown, 1999). There are two philosophical research approaches to ontology and epistemology: positivism and interpretivism (Hudson & Ozanne, 1988).

The positivist ontology sees the world external with an objective reality. Positivist research focuses on the description and explanation of the researched phenomena, and the researches tries to stay apart from the participants in the conducted research. Furthermore, the researcher uses a rational and consistently approach and his thought is governed by the hypothesis and theory of the conducted research (Carson, 2001).

Research using an interpretive philosophy do not use a well-structured research framework and assume that the reality is multiple and relative. Researches are involved in their research and they accept influence from their experience or from science. Interpretive research tries to understand the human behavior like reasons and meanings instead of and individual instead of making generalizations (Hudson & Ozanne, 1988).

Qualitative research is often considered to be using always an interpretative research philosophy, which is not true. As described by Hudson and Ozanne(1988) and Carson(2001) there are more factors that determine the used philosophy than the type of research method. The focus of this thesis is to describe and explain threats to data integrity in blockchain based data management systems, which is by following the previous described definitions[10] a positivistic philosophy.

3.4 Content Analysis

Textual data can be analyzed from different angles. One way is a statistical analysis of the data by utilizing text mining practices like n-grams, sentiment analysis, word count and many more. This approach is not suitable to analyze interview data in a way to get information out of it to answer the proposed research question. Therefore, an analysis of the content of the transcribed focus interviews is conducted.

---

[10] Full list of examples for positivism / interpretivism by Carson (2001, p. 6)

There are different approaches described in literature how to conduct such an analysis. For this research the qualitative content analysis approach by Mayring(2000) is used. Other publications on analyzing textual data are Braun and Clarke(2006) or Neuendorf(2010), which are similar to Mayrings approach.

The reason for choosing the qualitative content analysis by Mayring is because this approach reinforces that the creation of themes is done close to the data, which other approaches don't do.

According to Mayring(2000) qualitative content analysis can be applied to any kind of fixed communication such as minutes, transcribes, videos etc. but also includes content on other levels such as behavior and gestures. Mayring(2000) defines qualitative content analysis as:

> "[...] an approach of empirical, methodological controlled analysis of texts within
> their context of communication, following content analytical rules and step by step
> models, without rash quantification."

Within text analysis, the collected data is assigned to categories. In literature there are two distinct ways described how to create these categories or also called themes. Inductive theme creation is data driven and the categories or themes are created during the analysis of the data. The other approach is deductive category creation, where the themes are defined prior analyzing the data and then data is assigned to it (Boyatzis, 1998). The model developed by Mayring(2000) can be used for inductive and deductive category development. Within this research it is not possible to predefine categories, therefore an inductive category development approach is used. Mayring(2000) published a model, which is shown in Fig. 3., for using an inductive approach. The first step is to define the research question. The second step describes the determination of category definition and levels of abstraction for categories. Within the next step formulation of new categories are created by going through the data. In Step 4 a revision of the previous conducted steps is done, to ensure reliability and accuracy of the categories. This can be done after working through 10% to 50% of the data. After analyzing the rest of the collected data, another reliability check is done. As a last the results of the content analysis are interpreted. This can be done with quantitative steps for example frequency of appearance within the data.

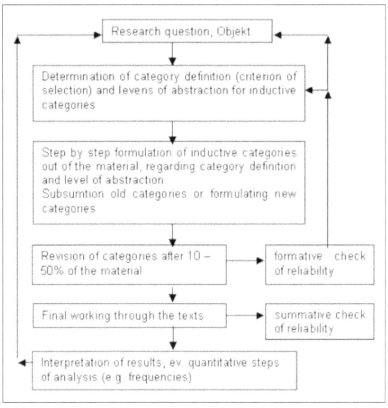

Figure 7: Inductive Category Development
(Mayring, 2000)

The analysis is conducted by using the tool QCAmap which available for free online[11]. This tool provides a supporting structure for developing categories. This tool also follows the Mayring (2000) approach which is also used within this thesis. QCAmap enables the author to define research questions, creating categories and setting up coding guidelines in an efficient way.

---

[11]   Link for QCAmap: https://www.qcamap.org

3.5 Data Presentation

This Chapter describes how the results of the data analysis are presented. There are three distinct visualizations for the results, one shows the found answers within the data, the second one summarizes the answers into categories, and the third one the frequency of the categories within the data.

As described by Mayring(2000) are the categories created within the analysis process of the data. The categories found, are recorded and described in a table with the following scheme, shown in Table 5. The category ID for the first research question start with D, while the answers related to the second research question are categorized with a C. The categories are created based on the transcribed interviews.

The following table shows how the identified categories are presented. The absolute frequency determines how often a category has been identified in the data. One category can be recorded more than once in a single interview,

Category ID	Category Name	Absolute Frequency
1	Low Adoption	3
2	Blockchain is not Mature	5

Table 5: Exemplary illustration of categories

3.6 Scientific Quality Criteria

According to Kirk and Miller(2005) high quality qualitative researched is determined by a high objectivity, reliability and validity. Objectivity can be seen as a heuristic assumption that all events in the universe can be explained by causality. In quality research, the objectivity can be evaluated by the researcher's validity and reliability. In research it is not possible to achieve a perfect validity, because not every aspect can be perfectly controlled. In qualitative research the problem of validity is if a researcher sees what he or she really sees. There are three various categories of validity: apparent validity, instrumental validity and theoretical validity. An apparent valid answer (to an interview question) is every correct answer. Instrumental validity is achieved when the used measuring instrument measures what it is supposed to. The third category of validity, theoretical or construct validity, is achieved when a measured variable represents the true meaning of the concept (Kirk & Miller, 2005).

Reliability in research can be distinguished in three different manifestations: quixotic, diachronic and synchronic. A measuring instrument that is quixotic reliable, delivers unchanged results, when the underlying variables are not changed. Diachronic reliability is the steadiness of results of an observation over time, while synchronic reliability refers to the similarity of observations within the same time period (Kirk & Miller, 2005).

To be able to conduct high quality research the author takes actions to enhance data validity and reliability. As previously described, this research will use qualitative data, collected during focus interviews, which is analyzed by using the qualitative content analysis, as published by Mayring (2000). The presented counter measures and problems in Table 6 are designed for this specific research project and may not be applicable for other research projects.

Quality Dimension	Problem	Counter measure
Apparent validity	Respondent gives wrong answer to one or more interview questions.	Data will be excluded in analysis
Instrumental validity	Questions do not give data that can answer the proposed research question	Third party review by advisor before data collection
Theoretical validity	The identified categories do not reflect the meaning of the collected data	A third party reviews the category creation
Quixotic reliability	The answers collected in an observation change, when the interview is repeated with the same questions.	Due to the semi-structed interview it is possible to answer in-depth questions to get all possible answers / perspectives
Diachronic reliability	An interviewee gives very different answers than other participants, because the time gap was very long, and technology has developed since then	All interviews are conducted within a specific period of 2 months.
Synchronic reliability	Answers to interview questions are like another observation that was conducted in a very similar timeframe.	Every interview is conducted individually without any third-party present, that also participates in the research

Table 6: Measures to enhance research quality

Every participant had to sign a consent sheet, with that he agrees to participate in the described research. These papers are not published and are only accessibly by the author. An exemplary consent sheet is attached in Appendix 4.

4 Results for Risk Identification

This Chapter will discuss the first results of this thesis, the identified risks and the security differences between public and private systems. The author conducted six interviews to collect data for the first and second research question. Based on the interview data 11 risks have been identified. For the second research questions 7 differences between public and private systems regarding data integrity have been identified.

4.1 Interview Participants

The following Table 7 shows a summary of the interview participants. Included is their profession /relation to blockchain technology and their country of residence. As explained earlier all data is anonymized. The participant id is not related to the sequence of the interviews or to interview id.

Participant	Profession	Country of Residence
1	Professor	USA
2	Blockchain Developer	Singapore
3	Professor	Austria
4	Blockchain Advisor	USA
5	IT-Consultant	Germany
6	Found of a blockchain startup	Austria

Table 7: Interview Participants

4.2 Identified Risks

In the following Table 8 the identified threats / risks are listed. The first column represents the category ID, the second column the title of the category. The absolute frequency indicates the number of marked passages in the data for each category. A category can be mentioned more than once during an interview, therefore the absolute frequency is in some cases higher than the number of conducted interviews. The absolute frequency is only used as an indicator how often a certain category is in the data set, but there are no results based on this variable.

Category	Category Title	Absolute Frequency
D1	Consensus Attack (51% Attack)	4
D2	Low Quality Smart Contract Code	3
D4	Alternative Chain	4

Category	Category Title	Absolute Frequency
D5	Misuse of Private Key	3
D6	Incorrect Data Input	5
D8	A blockchain contains historical data	2
D9	Node is malicious / out of sync	8
D11	Data on the blockchain cannot be deleted	2
D13	No Central Authority	2
D14	Trust in Protocol Developers	6
D15	Trust in Third Parties	3

Table 8:Identified Threats to Data Integrity in Blockchain Systems

4.3 Differences in Public and Private Blockchains

Within public and private blockchain systems 7 major differences regarding data integrity have been identified. Table 9 shows the results of the identified differences in private and public design. The absolute frequency for each category is listed, but it does not impact the results.

Category	Category Title	Absolute Frequency
C1	Different Consensus Models	2
C2	Higher Quality Code on Private Chains	2
C3	Public chains are more often target of a consensus attack	1
C4	Private chains can readjust itself easier	1
C5	Public chains are more reliable	1
C6	Only Known Parties on the Network	1
C7	Data is Private	1

Table 9: Differences Public & Private Systems

5 Discussion / Explanation of identified Risks and Differences

This Chapter will discuss / explain the results presented in the previous Chapter. While the first part focuses on the identified risks, the second part covers the differences between public and private systems.

5.1 Identified Risks

By discussing the identified risks / threats the research question 1 "What are the threats to data integrity within a blockchain system?" is considered as answered. When comparing the results to a the previous study about blockchain risks by Li et al.(2017), there are some differences but also similarities. The identified risks D1 and D2 have been also identified by Li et al.(2017), but all other risks are not in the mentioned study, due to the specialization on data integrity of this thesis.

5.1.1 Consensus Attack (51% Attack)

This risk is already widely-known among blockchain experts and in literature. Despite its name it is not really necessary to control 51% of the mining power to successfully conduct this attack. According to Antonopoulos(2015) this attack is possible when controlling about 30% of the total mining power. When an entity controls the majority of the mining power he/she is able to publish wrong blocks which can contain wrong data, which threatens the integrity of the data on the blockchain. This risk has also been identified by Li et al.(2017).

5.1.2 Poor Contract Code

The poor quality of contract code is often not really considered, and what repercussions bad code can have on users and ecosystems. Especially in public systems where everybody can deploy Smart Contracts (for example on Ethereum) it cannot be ruled out, that some poorly written code exists. There are several sources of error for example could the code just contain some syntax or spelling errors. Another possibility would be the missing implementation of error handling and therefore producing an invalid result on the blockchain (Personal Interview, Interview 6). A major example of poorly written smart contract code is the DAO incident which happened in 2016. Poorly written contract code threatens the correctness, completeness and validity of the data stored on the blockchain. A similar risk has also been identified by Li et al.(2017).

5.1.3 Alternative Chain

It is possible that there is a fork on the blockchain and more than one chain is existing. This can have several reasons. The first possibility is that somebody wants to change to protocol and challenge to original chain. This happened already several times to bitcoin where people forked it to bitcoin unlimited or bitcoin XT. The most recent and successful for of bitcoin is Bitcoin Cash, which was forked at block #478559 on August 1st 2017. Such forks always threaten the ecosystem of the blockchain and can mislead new users because they don't know which chain is the "real" one. Another scenario of an alternative chain is an inadvertent fork of the blockchain. This can happen if 2 miners find a new block of the chain at the same time and propagate it to the network (Personal Interview, Interview 1). Most of the time this threat only exists for a short time, because if another block is found the longer chain (which has more PoW done) is the valid chain (Personal Interview, Interview 6). Although the block which has no child block can lead to issues, for example when transferring coins. A lot of institutions (for example cryptocurrency exchanges) require more than one confirmation on transactions (depending on the value of the transaction) (Antonopoulos, 2015). This is not possible on the bitcoin network when a block does not have a direct successor. An alternative chain is a risk to the correctness and completeness of the data stored on the blockchain.

5.1.4 Misuse of Private Key

In blockchain systems, users rely on PKI (Public key infrastructures) to generate their public and private key. As described in Chapter 2.2.2 the public key is the address of an account or the address is derived from the public key. Beside financial transactions blockchains are also used for identity management, within projects like Civic. A misuse cannot only lead to loss of financial funds but also to identity theft and much more (Personal Interview, Interview 6) (Personal Interview, Interview 1). When an individual is misusing a private key the integrity of the data is reduced because of the risk to authorization and validation.

5.1.5 Incorrect Data Input

When storing data into a database there are often rules on how and what data to store, however it is possible in most systems that wrong data can be stored on the database, even though there are mechanisms in place to prevent it. When using blockchain systems such mechanism are often missing and therefore there is an increased chance of storing incorrect data in the blockchain (Personal Interview,

Interview 2). A blockchain is under normal circumstances an immutable data store, therefore it is not possible to remove data that is incorrect (Personal Interview, Interview 3). On the bitcoin blockchain, before a transaction gets confirmed is checked against several rules. This process prevents a lot of wrong data to be published on the blockchain network. On some blockchains it is possible to include profanities. For example, in bitcoin this data is stored in the coinbase (not to be confused with the exchange) part of a block. There are several marriage proposals on the bitcoin blockchain, which are not relevant for the operating of bitcoin and can be considered as wrong data[12] .

5.1.6 A blockchain contains historical data

Most of the time data on blockchain nowadays is transactional data of cryptocurrencies. If there is no update transaction the data on the blockchain is outdated. Because there is all the historical data stored in the blockchain, an older state of the data is seen as the most current one (Personal Interview, Interview 2). For every update of a value a transaction has to be approved. The historical data threatens the timeliness of the data and therefore reduces the degree of achieved data integrity.

5.1.7 Malicious node

When using a blockchain most users don't run their own full nodes to participate in the network. Most of them run a software access the blockchain on a node, which saves a lot of computing and storage. Public blockchains are mostly designed to be trustless, but when connected to a node the user trusts somebody. This node can of course act malicious. For example, could the node be not synchronized to the rest of the blockchain networks, therefore you could see an outdated version of the blockchain (Personal Interview, Interview 1). This threatens the timeliness of data and reduces the degree of achieved data integrity. As described by Antonopoulos(2015, pp. 199–204) block propagation is not real time, simply because there are physical limitation in network transmission. Another possibility is that the node provides the user that are connected to a fake blockchain. This can only happen in combination with a malicious wallet (Personal Interview, Interview 3) (Personal Interview, Interview 6). In this case the correctness and completeness of the data is compromised.

---

[12] https://blockchair.com/bitcoin/block/416236

5.1.8 Data on the blockchain cannot be deleted

As explained in point 5.1.6 a blockchain contains the whole history of the data on the blockchain. Therefore, once something is stored in a blockchain it is almost impossible to revoke it. In most cases this is an advantage for the blockchain technology (when thinking of financial transactions), but if there is some data stored on the chain that shouldn't be there this is a problem for the owner and/or publisher of the data. For example, if confidential data from a government is published on public blockchain this data is visible as long as the blockchain network is alive (Personal Interview, Interview 3). Data which cannot be deleted constitute a risk to the validity and accuracy of the stored data.

5.1.9 No Central Authority

When conducting a traditional financial transaction with a bank account there is a central authority (e.g. the bank) which is responsible for processing it. A public blockchain has a decentralized organization / politics (see Chapter 2.1), so there cannot be made a single entity made responsible for processing or fulfilling a transaction. When conducting a bitcoin transaction most of the time the sender will type the receiving address and then send the amount of bitcoin he wants to. An address in the bitcoin ecosystem is 27 to 34 characters long and includes a mixture of letters and numbers. When a typing mistake is made the transaction is send anyway and the chances are high that the funds are lost. There is no authority to call or contact to undo the transaction and send the funds back (Personal Interview, Interview 4). This pattern also applies to errors in the system (in the blockchain protocol), where there is often no central authority which can decide on how to fix a certain problem. And if there is such a powerful authority the next risk "Trust in Protocol Developers" has to be taken into consideration. When no central authority approves transactions, data or executed contracts on the blockchain the validity, authorization and correctness of the data is threatened.

5.1.10 Trust in Protocol Developers

A lot of blockchain projects struggling with decentralized governance (Personal Interview, Interview 6). The protocol developers maintaining the code have a lot of power in the ecosystem. In some cases, those figureheads and coders of leading projects have the possibility to let the organization act in their own interest (Personal Interview, Interview 4). For example, in 2016 after the DAO hack, the Ethereum team decided to fork the blockchain to restore the stolen funds to its user.

While this may sound good, people argue that is breaks the basic tenets of a public blockchain (Falkon, 2017). When looking at the bitcoin protocol developers there can be seen that only a handful of them contribute to code regularly and therefore have a lot of power in the ecosystem[13].Other blockchain projects try to tackle this problem by setting up a more decentralized governance and development structure consisting of known parties[14].

5.1.11 Trust in other Third Parties

Bitcoin was designed as a peer-2-peer payment system, however nowadays this not always the case. Especially in the world of cryptocurrencies most people use exchanges like Bitfinex for buying and selling coins. Therefore, a lot of people rely on those third parties when making transactions (Personal Interview, Interview 4). A lot of organizations are already aware of that and decentralized exchanges are upcoming. Another problem with cryptocurrency exchanges is the key management. All centralized exchanges don't give access to the private key, of an account. Therefore, a user has to trust the exchange that they are not signing any authorized transactions without their knowledge (Personal Interview, Interview 6). Exchanges can threaten the authorization and validity of the data on the blockchain / transaction by misusing their users' keys. Wallets can be published by various vendors, and are not always from the same organization as the blockchain itself (Antonopoulos, 2015). Therefore, there is also trust needed in the developer of the third-party wallet. A fraudulent wallet threatens the correctness and completeness of the data on the blockchain.

5.2 Differences public and private blockchains

The second research question of this thesis was "How do threats to data integrity differ in public and private blockchain systems?", which will be answered in this part. Each difference will be elaborated in more detail in this section.

5.2.1 Different Consensus Models

Blockchain systems can use different consensus algorithms and models (Chapter 2.2.5). Most consensus algorithms are mature cryptographic functions such as SHA256 is, which have been analyzed for security risks many times, for example by

---

[13]   https://github.com/bitcoin/bitcoin/graphs/contributors
[14]   https://www.cardano.org/en/home/

Kanade et al.(2004) or Gilbert and Handschuh(2004). It can be said that public blockchains use different consensus algorithms and/or methods than private systems (Personal Interview, Interview 1) (Personal Interview, Interview 3). For the author it was not possible to determine, based on the collected data, if this is an advantage for either of the one system designs.

5.2.2 Higher Quality Code on Private Chains

The quality of smart contract code on private chains is higher quality than on public systems (Personal Interview, Interview 1). When considering the architecture of the 2 designs, the private one only allows known party operating on the blockchain network and therefore also publishing and executing code. While in public systems every individual or organization can set up a smart contract anonymous. A higher quality of smart contracts leads to less wrong / incomplete data on the blockchain, which improves the degree of achieved data integrity.

5.2.3 Public chains are more often a target of a 51% attack

When talking about 51% attacks it always should be considered who could have interest to alter the blockchain. On a public blockchain a major asset owner could have the interest to alter the blockchain to his / her advantage (Personal Interview, Interview 3). In private systems all network participants know each other, so an attacker could be easily identified. This result lead to an advantage of private blockchain systems when it comes to 51% attacks.

5.2.4 Private chains can readjust itself easier

If problems occur with the state of the blockchain as explained in Chapter 5.1.10 with the DAO hack, a private chain can resolve such an issue easier (Personal Interview, Interview 4). Because all the participants on the private blockchain network know and trust each other, they can work out a solution in the best interest of its users. Therefore, a private chain can restore the valid state of the blockchain easier than a private one hence increases data integrity.

5.2.5 Public chains are more reliable

The general assumption in this case is that public chains are more reliable because of the larger number of participants on the network (Personal Interview, Interview 6). A higher number of miners results in mining power distribution and therefore reduces the risk that a single party controls 51% or more of the total mining power. The reduced risk of 51% attacks gives an advantage to the public blockchain design.

A reduced likelihood of a consensus attack can help to achieve better data integrity by avoiding wrong data by a party on the network that controls the majority of the mining power.

5.2.6 Only known parties on the network

According to Bashir(2018) a private blockchain is a form of a permissioned block-chain, therefor the participants on the blockchain network know and trust each other. For example, the bitcoin and Ethereum blockchains are designed to work trustless, which private chains don't necessarily have to. Because every participant knows each other on the network there may be a reduced chance that an entity publishes wrong or inaccurate information on purpose.

5.2.7 Data is private

The data on a public blockchain is visible to everybody, on a private chain this is not the case (Personal Interview, Interview 5). This allows private blockchains to deal with confidential data which should not be accessible by the public. This increases the integrity of the data on the private chain when compared to a public system.

6 Quantitative Research Methodology

This Chapter will describe the second empirical part of this thesis. The results from the previous step are identified threats, and within this part, this data will be evaluated numerical to be able to prioritize it. The data used is quantitative in nature and will be collected via an online survey. In the first part personal interviews are used, which would be also a suitable data collection method for quantitative data, but in this case not really suitable. Cooper and Schindler(2014) differentness between three different types of interview types for business research: Self-Administered Survey, Phone Interview and Personal Interview. The first research method utilized personal interviews (but in a qualitative manner). These types of interviews are very time consuming and it takes a long time to find suitable interview partners. To gain quantitative data it would take too long to conduct personal interviews for this specific master thesis and is therefore not an appropriate method. Phone Surveys offer the advantage that they are much faster to conduct, and they are more time and location independent. But participants are often not willing to talk to strangers on the phone, and the target group for this research may not be always available via phone. The third method is self-administered surveys that can be send out via mail or distributed via the internet. This option is very cheap and timely flexible. Online surveys also offer a high degree of anonymity which is very important to participants, although such surveys often suffer a low response rate (Cooper & Schindler, 2014). Other methods of quantitative data collection are not considered, because the objective is to collect empirical data, which has not available yet.

After assessing the three types of surveys the author decided to conduct a self-administrated survey that is distributed online.

6.1 Online Survey Design

A survey is a tool for collecting data and is often used as a synonym for questionnaire. Questionnaires are a part of a survey, but the whole process of a survey ranges from goal definition to conducting the analysis (Dillman, 2000)(Sue & Ritter, 2007).

The design is based on the survey process illustrated by Sue and Ritter(2007) The questionnaire is impacted by ISO27005:2011 Chapter 8, because it delivers the necessary methodology for the questionnaire design. The survey is hosted on Google Forms. This service uses automatic translation for the user interface (e.g.

Buttons) which is helpful when conducting research with international participants.

6.1.1 Defining Objectives

The goal of this survey is to gain information about data integrity threats in blockchain systems. The survey aims to identify the risks with the highest estimated risk. The potential audience of this survey are individuals and organizations that want to implement any system that utilized blockchain technology.

6.1.2 Population & Sampling Size

The term population in relation to a survey is the group of entities that share a set of characteristics, while a sample is a subset of the population. The purpose of a sample is to allow and estimation of a characteristic on the defined population (Zikmund, 2009).

There can be no clear number defined how big the population of the survey is. Therefore, an estimation has to be made. To make an estimation of potential individuals that are interested in introducing a blockchain system in an organization the professional social network linkedIn.com is used. LinkedIn allows its users to form groups of interest and discuss current topics and much more. The following social media groups in Table 10 have been considered as relevant, because those are the biggest regarding blockchain technology and the members are quite active:

Group Name on linkedIn.com	Members (By June 2018)
Blockchain Professionals & Developers	7,472
Blockchain, Distributed Ledgers and Smart Contracts for Business	11,171
Blockchain & Distributed Ledger Technology (DLT)	12,815
Average	**10,486**

Table 10: Considered LinkedIn Groups

But not all group participants are IT professionals that are targeted, and users can be members of multiple groups, therefore the author makes a best guess based on the previous numbers and defines population size as 5,000.

When defining a sample size, it is important to know beforehand what kind of sample is used for the survey. In general, there can be differentiated between probability samples and nonprobability samples. The major difference is that in probability every sampling unit is selected randomly and has a fair chance of selection, while non-probability sampling selects its sampling units arbitrarily. Non-probability sampling is used for exploratory research that generates a hypothesis, rather than testing it (Zikmund, 2009).

This survey uses nonprobability sampling because it probability sampling is not suitable for this kind of research. Also, a fair chance for every participant of the population cannot be guaranteed, and a total list of the population is not available. The sample size in nonprobability samples are not determined by a formula like within a probability sample. The minimum sample size is 30, but it should be as large as possible (Alreck & Settle, 2004). Based on literature this surveys sample size is minimum 30 but aims to archive more respondents if possible, to increase the accuracy and reliability of the results.

6.1.3 Data Collection Strategy

This survey uses a combination of convenience sampling and judgment sampling for its data collection. Also, will the survey use an incentive for participants to increase the number of responses. This incentive will be a lottery where every participant can voluntary provide his email address to win a voucher for a major online retailer with the value of 10€ or any equivalent available currency. According to Martinsson, Dumitrescu, and Riedel(2016) financial incentives are the best working incentives when conducting a survey. The winner will be selected with a random number generator, which gives back one of the numbers of the response ids. The winner will be selected via a single mail. All provided addresses will be held confidential and deleted after this step.

Convenience sampling is to make people participate in your survey that are convenient available. But it also considers economic factors when talking about convenient. Although selected samples may be not representative, because of the selection process. The survey also uses judgement sampling which is a process where an individual select samples based on their knowledge and experience (Zikmund, 2009).

This online survey will be distributed in various social media groups that are focusing on blockchain and its related disciplines. Furthermore, the author will invite individuals based on their characteristics and knowledge in the required field to participate in the survey.

6.1.4 Designing the survey questions

When developing survey question, it is essential to formulate precise and simple questions. Questions have to be neutral formulated otherwise the answers are biased, because the questions are leading or loaded. Also, a very common practice is questionnaires is to start with more general questions and then use the funnel technique to more specific questions (Zikmund, 2009). Therefore, the questionnaire will start with a main information page to brief the users, followed by simple demographics and then focus on the main questions which are necessary to collect data for the research.

The only relevant demographic data within this research is age, education and employment. This data will enhance the research quality by providing more details about the survey participants. Bradburn, Sudman, and Wansink(2004) defined more categories such as gender, marital status, race and origin but this data is not needed for the conducted research. For the creation of the demographic questions the guideline by Bradburn et al.(2004) is used, which is also used by the U.S. Census Bureau. This results in the following survey questions:

What is your age?

Numeric answer

What is your highest degree you received?

Answering by choosing one of the following categories:

- None
- Elementary school diploma
- High school diploma or the equivalent (GED)
- Associate degree
- Bachelor's degree
- Master's degree
- Professional degree (MD, DDS, DVM, LLB, JD, DD)
- Doctorate degree (Ph.D. or Ed.D.)

What is your current occupation?

Text Answer

As stated in earlier the risk analysis is based on ISO27005 and therefore the questions have to be compliant with this standard. ISO27005 evaluates the consequences and the likelihood of a risk, therefore every risk will be evaluated by these two criteria's. As described earlier ISO27005 supports qualitative and quantitative measurements, but in this survey a quantitative approach will be used with a scale from 1 to 10. When doing ratings an ordinal scale is mostly used. This type of scale is also able to deliver the necessary data to perform the desired descriptive statistics (median and range). Furthermore, an ordinary scale does not give the distance between two data points, which mean in a risk rated with a likelihood with 8/10 is not double as likely to happen as a risk with a rating of 4/10. A ratings scale from 1 to 5 is often used, but to be able to generate more precise results the scale has been set with a range from 1 to 10 (Zikmund, 2009). To make it easier for respondents, the highest and lowest value have a qualitative description. All of the previously identified eleven risks are in the survey. There is a section for rate all likelihood questions and a section for to rate the consequences of all the risks. The final survey questions can be seen in Appendix 2. An overview of the used logic of the questions provides Figure 8. The number on each box indicates the section number and question number (only where necessary). The brighter boxes (orange) indicate optional parts. When a participant does not complete all steps of the survey there is no record created.

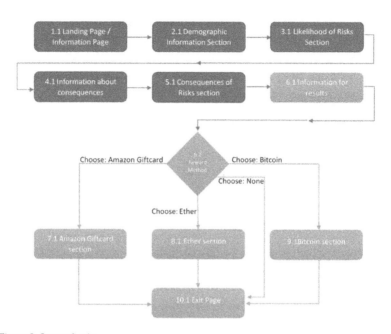

Figure 8: Survey Logic

6.2 Data Analysis &Visualization

The data analysis for this survey is quite simple, because there are no correlations of variables measured. The goal of the analysis is to find out the average rating for each identified risk, therefore the mean and median are applicable. The median measures give the 50th percentile or also the midpoint of the dataset, while the mean represents the arithmetic average. The mean is influenced by exceptional values (outliers), in contrast to the median (Zikmund, 2009). Therefore, all results to the questions will be analyzed by calculating the median of each individual question, and dimension. Other measurements that are part of the descriptive statistic will be calculated depending on the available data. For each demographic variable a graph will be created.

To calculate the risk score of each individual threat, the sum of likelihood and consequence is calculated. In this case the sum is a valid measurement because according to ISO27005 both dimensions are weighted the same in the risk evaluation process. Depending on the sum it can be categorized in one of the following priority categories.

The categories described in Table 11 are good practice in risk evaluation, because ISO27005 defines no clear qualitative measurements this 5-category scheme is used. The visualization will be done in R Studio where a boxplot for each dimension (likelihood and consequences) is created. An overview of the risks will be visualized in a scatterplot where likelihood and consequences are the axis. Depending on the results any further visualizations may be added. The used code for the visualization is in the Appendix 3.

Category	Very Low	Low	Medium	High	Very High
Risk Score	< 4	4 – 7.99	8 – 11.99	12 -15.99	16 <

Table 11: Risk Priority Categories

6.3 Scientific Quality Criteria

The ensure a high standard of research quality, the survey is pretested. Pretesting is approach when developing surveys, where the researcher takes several iterative steps to rewrite and revise parts of the survey. This is especially necessary when a survey includes complex questions, which may be not understandable in the same way for each participant. But also other properties like response rate can be determined when using pretesting. (Zikmund, 2009).

This survey has been pretested with five individuals. The main intent of this pretest was to get feedback for the wording of the risks/scenarios. This pretesting setting took place in a group meeting. By using the guideline of Zikmund(2009) the following topics have been addressed during the pretest.

Questionnaire Format

The survey is conducted self-administrated and hosted on Google Forms. This tool is a very common choice among research surveys. Nobody of the pretesting group struggled with this tool during the test.

Questionnaire Flow

To achieve satisfactory results with a survey a good flow and logic of the questions is important. The questions in the survey have been split into three main parts: Questions regarding likelihood, consequences and a third part for the lottery. According to the participants in the pretest the flow was well designed, but there have been some logic errors in the survey. This means the planned logic, when choosing the payment method, a participant can choose (for the incentive) the routing was wrong. This error would have led to some aborted submissions and was therefore changed immediately in the Google Form.

Clear and easy questions

Within the pretest participants struggled with rating two scenarios. For the identified risks D8 and D11 (seen in Chapter 4) the participants were not able to understand the problem and rating regarding likelihood and consequences. Pretester's agreed that those are valid threats, but those threats are not really able to be rated regarding likelihood, because these events are certain to happen. Therefore, those two risks have been rated with a likelihood of 10/10 and only the consequences for data integrity are rated by the survey participants.

7 Results for Risk Evaluation

In this Chapter the author will share the results of the risk evaluation. All of the 11 previously identified risks have been rated according to likelihood of occurrence and the consequences for data integrity. Overall 41 valid responses have been collected during the 2 weeks' timeframe, where the survey was online available.

7.1 Survey Participants

This section provides information about the individuals that participated in the survey. Figure 9 shows the age of the participants, with a range from 22 to 51. The median age of the 41 participants is 28 years. 26 years is the most common age with a total count of 6.

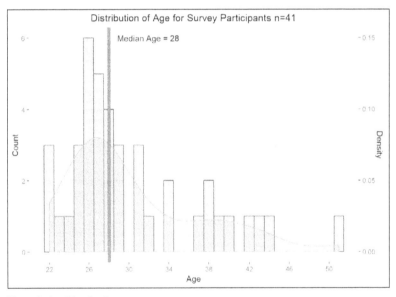

Figure 9: Age Distribution

The Figure 10 provides information about the highest degree every participant has occupied. 16 participants have obtained a Masters degree as their highest education, 15 a Bachelors degree, 5 a Ph.D., 4 an associate degree and 1 a high school diploma or equivalent.

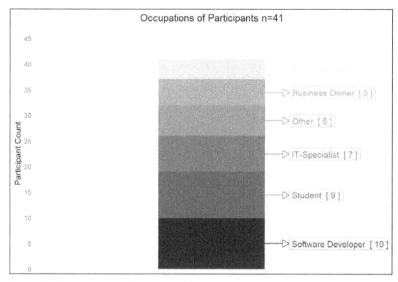

Figure 10: Highest degree of Survey Participants

Figure 11 shows the occupation for each survey participant. Most participants were Software Developers (10) followed by Students (9), IT-Specialists (7), Other (6), Business Owners (5) Consultants (4). The provided data has been standardized to fit in one of those categories.

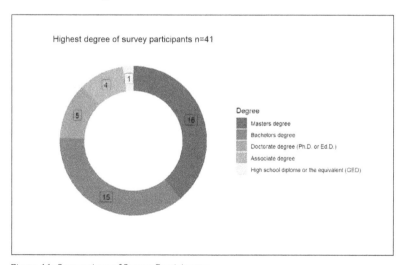

Figure 11: Occupations of Survey Participants

7.2 Research Results

The following Figure 12 shows the results of the survey regarding the likelihood of the described risks. This illustration shows the minimum, maximum, all 4 quartiles and the median.

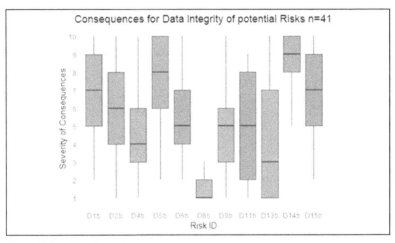

Figure 12: Likelihood of Risks

In Figure 13 the results are shown for the potential consequences of the identified threats in Chapter 4 The highest median has threat D14 followed by D5.

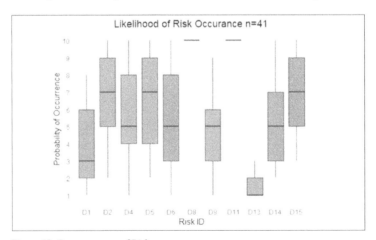

Figure 13: Consequences of Risks

In the following Table 12 the numerical results of the previous visualizations are shown. Those values are necessary for the following graphs and the final categorization. These values will be visualized in a matrix in Figure 14.

Category	Likelihood (Median)	Consequences (Median)	Risk Score	Risk Rating
D1	3	7	10	Medium
D2	7	6	13	High
D4	5	4	9	Low
D5	7	8	15	High
D6	5	5	10	Medium
D8	10^{15}	1	11	Medium
D9	5	5	10	Medium
D11	10^{16}	5	15	High
D13	1	3	4	Low
D14	5	9	14	High
D15	7	7	14	High

Table 12: Numerical Results for each Category

Within Figure 14 the previously measured dimensions are brought together. Also, the rating mechanism as described in Chapter 3.2.5 is applied to be able to categorize the threats / risks into their categories. A small jitter has been added to the graphic to show 2 datapoints for D6 and D9. One of the total 11 identified threats has a low risk rating, while 5 of them are medium and 5 are high rated. None of the identified risks have been classified in the categories "Very Low" and "Very High". The risks D11 and D5 got highest rated with a score of 15/20. D13 is rated the lowest with 4/20.

---

[15] Predefined rating (see previous Chapter)
[16] Predefined rating (see previous Chapter)

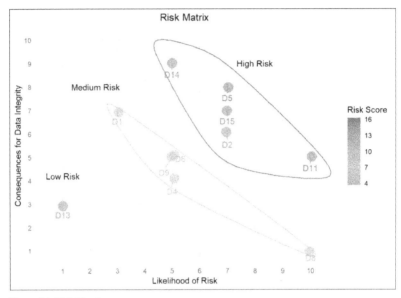

Figure 14: Risk Matrix

An in-depth discussion of the results and their implications on public blockchain systems is done in the following Chapter.

8 Discussion & Implications of the Results from the Risk Evaluation

This Chapter will discuss the results of the ratings for each risk. Also, the implications for blockchain technology and how to reduce some of these risks are explained in this section.

8.1 Discussion

In the previous Chapter the findings have been presented. In this Chapter these results are interpreted and briefly discussed. This part answers the last research question, how the previous identified risks are rated among likelihood and their consequences.

D1 – 51% Attack

The risk D1 has an overall risk rating of "Medium", while scoring 3/10 at likelihood and 7/10 in Consequences. As discussed earlier the attacker does not need 51% of the mining power to be successful with the attack, it can also be around 30%. According to Bach, Mihaljevic, and Zagar(2018) the power consumption of bitcoin in February 2018 was about 50.08TWh/year, which is close to the power consumption of Portugal (49.8 TWh/year) and Uzbekistan (51.3 TWh/year). Despite the high-power consumption, it is necessary to obtain the mining hardware. An exact cost estimation for the hardware cost is quite difficult because the availability and pricing for specialized application-specific integrated circuit (ASIC) miners is constantly changing. The bitcoin information platform GoBitcoin.io estimates hardware cost in the range of US$ 2.8 billion (30% mining power) to US$6.8 billion (51% mining power).

The currently biggest public blockchain (highest market capitalization) utilizing PoS is Cardano (see Chapter 2.2.5). To acquire 51% would cost several billion US$, further the supply on exchanges and other markets must be high enough so be able to acquire all these tokens.

D2 – Poor Contract Code

This risk scores 7/10 in likelihood and 6/10 in consequences. The possibility that everybody can create smart contracts on a public blockchain increases the likelihood of this risk. It has happened already several times that bad code in smart contract lead to the loss of funds or similar. Measuring the consequence of smart contract code is quite difficult. Andresen(2018) gives a nice overview of recent problems and hacks of smart contracts. According to this article problems in widely used smart contracts have resulted in the loss of hundreds of million dollars, but a rarely used contract may have legible to no consequences at all. Therefore, the risk of bad smart contract code is depending a lot on its purpose and on the amount of expected executions.

D4 – Alternative Chain

The results for this risk are 5/10 in likelihood and 4/10 in consequences which leads to an overall rating of medium risk. The likelihood of an inadvertent fork is depending on the used chain, mining difficulty, block time and other parameters. In 2016 the rate of such "uncle blocks" are 6 to 8 percent of the total blocks on the Ethereum blockchain (Buterin, 2016). On the Ethereum blockchain these blocks are still included as uncles, but other chains they are not, and therefore the transactions inside this block have only one confirmation. As explained earlier some services require more than one confirmation and therefore be not working as expected.

D5 – Misuse of Private Key

The misuse of private keys has a likelihood rating of 7/10 and the consequences are rated 8/10. To prevent a misuse of a private key it must be stored safely. By obtaining a private key the related account can be accessed anytime from anywhere. According to Lai and LEE Kuo Chuen(2018) the use of a an hardware security module (HSM) to store private keys because then the key is never visible because it never leaves the module.. According to Franco(2015) there are plenty of attacking scenarios to steal private keys from user. Every theft of a private key result in a total loss of control of the account.

D6 – Incorrect Data Input

This risk is rated overall medium and was evaluated with 5/10 in likelihood and the same in consequences. As explained earlier blockchain systems are often missing mechanisms that prevent malicious data to be published. Although systems like bitcoin use rulesets to verify transactions are therefor prevent the publication of wrong data. The consequences in the event of publishing wrong data very depends on the data itself.

D8 – A blockchain contains historical data

That risk that a blockchain stores historical data has been rated with 1/10 in consequences and 10/10 in likelihood. The likelihood was predefined, as mentioned earlier. When data is updated on a blockchain a transaction is executed which is always timestamped. Therefore, it is easy to determine if the current data on the chain is up to date or not.

D9 – Flawed Node

The risk of a malicious or that the node is out of sync node is rated with 5/10 in likelihood also 5/10 in consequences. As discussed earlier a node can be out of sync when the propagation time of a block is too high or when a fork of the chain occurs. The number of forks occurring is depending a lot on the predefined block time in the blockchain protocol Antonopoulos(2015). Unintentional forks last most of the time only for a few minutes resolve itself within the next few blocks (Personal Interview, Interview 4). A malicious node would be for example able to steal private keys and lead to more profound consequences than a node that is not synchronized to the rest of the network.

D11 – Data on the blockchain cannot be deleted

The risk D11 has been rated in the category "High" with the predefined likelihood of 10/10 and consequences of 5/10. There is a general consent in literature that blockchains are considered immutable, but there was no publication available, that addressed this property as a risk. Especially when considering secret information for governments or organizations this could lead to problems (Personal Interview, Interview 3). At the time of writing this thesis there are now proclamations that such an event occurred, and sensible data has been stored permanently on the blockchain.

D13 – Missing central authority leads to malfunction

The missing of a central authority has been rated the lowest among the identified risks, with likelihood of 1/10 and consequences of 3/10. There are no reports/publications available that the bitcoin network had any problems in the past due to the missing of a central authority. The intended purpose of bitcoin as the first blockchain is to remove central authorities and achieve consensus by using code. When sending a transaction which contains incorrect information (e.g. wrong recipient) the consequences for the user are high.

D14 – Protocol developer abuses its power

The risk of trusting in developers to maintain the code is rated with 5/10 in likelihood and 9/10 in consequences, which leads to a "High" overall rating. Protocol developers have in most cases interest in providing a flawless and well operation chain, because they are stakeholders. Of course, it cannot be ruled out that the power is used to drive certain decisions (as earlier explained in the DAO scenario). The consequences of a power abuse from the protocol developers are unpredictable and can vary from negligible to the discontinuation of the blockchain.

D15 – Third Party Failure

The risk of trusting third parties is evaluated with 7/10 in likelihood and 7/10 in consequences, which leads to an overall rating of "High". Events in the past showed that especially exchanges are vulnerable third parties. There have been more than 10 big failures / hacks within cryptocurrency exchanges, which lead to the loss of funds valued several billion US$ (Neuron, 2018). Some of these events happened also in the previous months, therefore the treat of a third-party failure is still visible. The failure of a cryptocurrency exchange brings also a big economical threat, but this kind of risks are not considered in this research.

8.2 Implications of Results

First this Chapter discusses the impact of the results, and how to manage the previously identified risks.

As explained in Chapter 2 one strength of a blockchain is data integrity. Although there have been several risks identified, it cannot be generalized that blockchains should be considered insecure. But to be able to deliver a well operating and secure public blockchain solution the identified risks must be considered, and their likelihood minimized.

Based on the results it can be said that large scale public blockchain are not very vulnerable to consensus attacks. But in small public environments the situation is different because obtaining 30% or 50% of the total mining power is not as difficult as in larger systems, independent if a blockchain uses PoW or PoS. The implementation of a DPoS could bring more security, through the involvement of all the users. DPoS is not widely adopted yet (see Table 2 in Chapter 2.2.5), therefore more in-depth experiences are missing, and it is far from perfect. The quality of smart contract code can be improved several ways. Standards are being defined (such as ERC20 or ERC721 on the Ethereum blockchain) and tools for code checks are available. Utilizing this tools and methods will improve the quality of code but does not guarantee perfect code. Forks can be unwittingly but also political motivated. As explained by Antonopoulos(2015) the block time has a major impact on the frequency of small forks that happen when a block is found by 2 parties at the same time. Reducing network delays can also lead to a reduced number of forks, because the block propagation time is reduced. Avoiding political forks (like Bitcoin Cash) must be resolved on governance level. Of course, everybody can make its own fork of public blockchain. But if there are no substantial benefits of the forking chain over the legacy blockchain it will be hard to convince users to switch. To avoid private key misuse a safe storage for private keys is necessary. As recommended by Lai and LEE Kuo Chuen(2018) a HSM is currently the safest option. Such devices are available for cryptocurrencies by companies like Trezor[17], Ledger[18] and some others. From a developer perspective it is necessary to implement a key creation procedure / management that avoids collisions. To avoid incorrect data and therefore threaten the integrity of a blockchain the design of the applications based on the blockchain is crucial. For example, mechanisms to check data before storing it permanent can improve the data quality. To prevent flawed nodes user should make sure the nodes are trustworthy they connect to. As a node operation it is essential to keep no node synchronized, which can be better achieved by reducing network delays and having security measures against DDoS attacks in place. A missing central authority can threaten the integrity of data on a blockchain because of the missing supervision. To reduce this risk the individuals or organization responsible for the blockchain must achieve a well-balanced governance model, that is decentralized but maintains the quality of a centralized authority. Prevent the abuse of the system by powerful parties such as protocol developers is difficult. If the public chain is tokenized the distribution of those tokens may indicate the power distribution in the blockchain environment. When talking about the power of third parties it should always be considered that most blockchain are designed P2P and if the use of the third-party service or product is necessary.

---

[17] https://trezor.io
[18] https://www.ledger.com

9 Limitations of the Research

Finding a perfect approach for conducting explorative research such as the author did in this thesis is very difficult. Therefore, in this Chapter explains the limitations that apply to the conducted research.

For data collection of the first empirical part experts on the field of blockchain have been interviewed. This method brings several limitations with it. At first no human being has total knowledge, therefor it could be possible that some risks have not been identified. There have been six interviews conducted, although the number of new identified risks declined with every interview, it cannot be ruled out that a higher number of high qualified participants would increase the number of identified risks. Also, some of the participants native language is not English, hence it can be not ruled out that some parts of the answers or questions are understood wrong. The data has been analyzed with the content analysis framework by Mayring. The use of a different analysis method may lead to different results. Also has the author utilized the online tool QCAMAP for the content analysis. If the analysis has been conducted with a different tool or without any IT tool the results may be different. The author worked as assiduously, precise and objective it cannot be ruled out that, if the analysis is conducted by somebody else the identified categories are different.

The second part used a quantitative approach to collect data. The survey had 41 participants and it cannot be ruled out that a higher number of participants would lead to the same results. The participants have different occupations and are differently aged. More than 50% of the participants are younger than 30 and are software developer or students. If the study had participants with a more widespread age range and more different occupations the results could be different. The survey was distributed online, therefor it was not possible for people without internet connection to participate. Further only members of topic specific social media groups got the possibility to participate in the survey. The survey used an ordinary scale for ratings from 1 to 10 which is not the standard in risk evaluation. The standard ISO27001 defines no clear standard for evaluations of risks, but often a scale from 1 to 5 is used. It cannot be ruled out that a different scale in the survey would have led to different research results. The results were analyzed using descriptive statistics (mean and range). A use of other measurements may lead to different results in the risk evaluation. The raw data from the survey has been analyzed using R and R Studio. Although the author worked as precise and assiduously as possible it cannot be ruled out there are syntax, spelling or logic errors in the data analysis. The results have been discussed using a current and complete set of literature, hence the use of any different literature may have given a different point of view on the identified risks.

10 Conclusion

This thesis identified and evaluated risks regarding data integrity on blockchain systems using Focus Interviews and a Survey. Overall there have been 11 risks identified regarding which can impact the data integrity on public blockchain systems. Further there have been 7 differences identified between public and private blockchain systems in the realm of data integrity. The findings of this thesis can be used by organizations as a guideline for increasing data integrity in a public blockchain system. The results for the differences in public and private systems, can be used as a tool to support the decision between public and private design.

The identified risks in this thesis do not identify blockchain technology as an unsecure technology. None of the identified risks have been classified as "Very High", but 5 risks have been rated "High", 4 with "Medium" and 1 with "Low" The identified risks have to taken into consideration and should be minimized in their likelihood of occurrence to maintain or improve data integrity. While there have been differences identified between public and private systems, based on this research it cannot be generalized that one of the systems designs is more secure than the other. With the future development some risks may disappear because new technologies are developed, but it is very difficult to forecast when this will happen.

There are several ways that this research can be extended through further conducted research. This thesis focused on public blockchain systems, while it is also necessary to identify the risks in private systems. The focus of this thesis is on data integrity. When considering the 3 major properties of data (confidentially, integrity, availability) further research can identify risks regarding confidentially and availability in blockchain systems.

11 References

Alreck, P. L., & Settle, R. B. (2004). *The survey research handbook* (3rd ed.). *McGraw-Hill/Irwin series in marketing*. Boston: McGraw-Hill/Irwin.

Andresen, M. (2018). The biggest smart contract hacks in history or how to endanger up to US $2.2 billion. Retrieved from https://medium.com/solidified/the-biggest-smart-contract-hacks-in-history-or-how-to-endanger-up-to-us-2-2-billion-d5a72961d15d

Andrews, G. R. (2000). *Foundations of multithreaded, parallel, and distributed programming*. Reading, Mass. u. a.: Addison Wesley.

Antonopoulos, A., & Wood, G. A. (2018). *Mastering Ethereum: Building smart contracts and dapps.*

Antonopoulos, A. M. (2015). *Mastering Bitcoin*. Sebastopol, CA: O'Reilly Media.

Bach, L. M., Mihaljevic, B., & Zagar, M. (2018). Comparative analysis of blockchain consensus algorithms. In *2018 41st International Convention on Information and Communication Technology, Electronics and Microelectronics (MIPRO)* (pp. 1545–1550). IEEE. https://doi.org/10.23919/MIPRO.2018.8400278

Back, A. (2002). Hashcash - A Denial of Service Counter-Measure. Retrieved from http://www.hashcash.org/papers/hashcash.pdf

Baran, P. (1964). *On Distributed Communications: Introduction to Distributed Communications Network*. Santa Monica, CA. Retrieved from https://www.rand.org/content/dam/rand/pubs/research_memoranda/2006/RM3420.pdf

Bashir, I. (2017). *Mastering Blockchain: Distributed ledgers, decentralization and smart contracts explained*. Birmingham, UK: Packt Publishing.

Bashir, I. (2018). *Mastering blockchain: Distributed ledger technology, decentralization, and smart contracts explained* (2. ed.). *Expert insight*. Birmingham: Packt Publishing Ltd.

Bayer, D., Haber, S., & Stornetta, W. S. (1993). Improving the Efficiency and Reliability of Digital Time-Stamping. In R. Capocelli, A. de Santis, & U. Vaccaro (Eds.), *Sequences II* (pp. 329–334). New York, NY: Springer New York. https://doi.org/10.1007/978-1-4613-9323-8_24

Boritz, J. E. (2005). IS practitioners' views on core concepts of information integrity. *International Journal of Accounting Information Systems*, *6*(4), 260–279. https://doi.org/10.1016/j.accinf.2005.07.001

Boyatzis, R. E. (1998). *Transforming qualitative information: Thematic analysis and code development*. Thousand Oaks, Calif.: Sage.

Bradburn, N. M., Sudman, S., & Wansink, B. (2004). *Asking Questions: The Definitive Guide to Questionnaire Design -- For Market Research, Political Polls, and Social and Health Questionnaires. Research Methods for the Social Sciences*. Hoboken: John Wiley & Sons Inc.

Brammertz, W., & Mendelowitz, A. I. (2018). From digital currencies to digital finance: The case for a smart financial contract standard. *The Journal of Risk Finance, 19*(1), 76–92. https://doi.org/10.1108/JRF-02-2017-0025

Braun, V., & Clarke, V. (2006). Using thematic analysis in psychology. *Qualitative Research in Psychology, 3*(2), 77–101. https://doi.org/10.1191/1478088706qp063oa

Buterin, V. (2014). A next-generation smart contract and decentralized application platform. Retrieved from https://github.com/ethereum/wiki/wiki/White-Paper#decentralized-autonomous-organizations

Buterin, V. (2016). Uncle Rate and Transaction Fee Analysis. Retrieved from https://blog.ethereum.org/2016/10/31/uncle-rate-transaction-fee-analysis/

Buterin, V. (2017). The Meaning of Decentralization. Retrieved from https://medium.com/@VitalikButerin/the-meaning-of-decentralization-a0c92b76a274

Carson, D. (2001). *Qualitative marketing research*. London, Thousand Oaks, Calif: Sage. Retrieved from http://search.ebscohost.com/login.aspx?direct=true&scope=site&db=nlebk&db=nlabk&AN=593394

Castro, M., & Liskov, B. (2002). Practical byzantine fault tolerance and proactive recovery. *ACM Transactions on Computer Systems, 20*(4), 398–461. https://doi.org/10.1145/571637.571640

Christin, N., & Safavi-Naini, R. (Eds.). (2014). *Financial Cryptography and Data Security. Lecture Notes in Computer Science.* Berlin, Heidelberg: Springer Berlin Heidelberg.

Cooper, D. R., & Schindler, P. S. (2014). *Business research methods* (12. edition). *The McGraw-Hill/Irwin series in operations and decision sciences Business statistics.* New York, NY: McGraw-Hill Irwin.

Dillman, D. A. (2000). *Mail and internet surveys: The tailored design method* (2. ed.). New York, NY: Wiley.

Dwork, C., & Naor, M. (1993). Pricing via Processing or Combatting Junk Mail. In E. F. Brickell (Ed.), *Lecture Notes in Computer Science: Vol. 740. Advances in cryptology - CRYPTO '92: 12th Annual International Cryptology Conference, Santa Barbara, California, USA, August 16 - 20, 1992 ; proceedings* (pp. 139–147). Berlin: Springer.

Easton, J. (2018, January 22). Blockchain Name Changes Are Still Paying Off. *Bloomberg Markets.* Retrieved from https://www.bloomberg.com/news/articles/2018-01-22/blockchain-name-changes-are-still-proving-fodder-for-stock-rally

Falkon, S. (2017). The Story of the DAO—Its History and Consequences. Retrieved from https://medium.com/swlh/the-story-of-the-dao-its-history-and-consequences-71e6a8a551ee

Franco, P. (2015). *Understanding Bitcoin: Cryptography, Engineering and Economics. The Wiley Finance Series.* Chichester, West Sussex: Wiley.

Gaetani, E., Aniello, L., Baldoni, R., Lombardi, F., Margheri, A., & Sassone, V. (Eds.) 2017. *Blockchain-based Database to Ensure Data Integrity in Cloud Computing Environments.*

Gilbert, H., & Handschuh, H. (2004). Security Analysis of SHA-256 and Sisters. In T. Kanade, J. Kittler, J. M. Kleinberg, F. Mattern, J. C. Mitchell, O. Nierstrasz,. . . R. J. Zuccherato (Eds.), *Lecture Notes in Computer Science. Selected Areas in Cryptography* (Vol. 3006, pp. 175–193). Berlin, Heidelberg: Springer Berlin Heidelberg. https://doi.org/10.1007/978-3-540-24654-1_13

Gillham, B. (2001). *Research Interview. Continuum Research Methods.* London: Continuum International Pub. Group.

Gillham, B. (2005). *Case study research methods* (Repr). *Real world research*. London: Continuum.

44 U.S.C. § 3542 - DEFINITIONS, Government Printing Office.

Grosch, H. R. J. (1953). High Speed Arithmetic: The Digital Computer as a Research Tool. *Journal of the Optical Society of America*, *43*(4), 306. https://doi.org/10.1364/JOSA.43.000306

Haber, S., & Stornetta, S. W. (1991). How to Time-Stamp a Digital Document. *Journal of Cryptology*, *3*(2), 99–111.

Houy, N. (2014). It Will Cost You Nothing to 'Kill' a Proof-of-Stake Crypto-Currency. *SSRN Electronic Journal.* Advance online publication. https://doi.org/10.2139/ssrn.2393940

Hudson, L. A., & Ozanne, J. L. (1988). Alternative Ways of Seeking Knowledge in Consumer Research. *Journal of Consumer Research*, *14*(4), 508. https://doi.org/10.1086/209132

International Organization for Standardization. (1994). Accuracy (trueness and precision) of measurement methods and results -- Part 1: General principles and definitions. Retrieved from https://www.iso.org/standard/11833.html

IOTA Foundation. (2018). What is IOTA. Retrieved from https://iota.readme.io/docs/what-is-iota

ISACA. (2012). *COBIT 5: A business framework for the governance and management of enterprise IT : an ISACA® framework*. Rolling Meadows, Ill.: ISACA.

ISO (2011, June 1). *Information technology - Security techniques - Information security risk management*. (ISO27005:2011).

ISO (2013, October 1). *Information technology - Security techniques -Information security management systems -Requirements*. (ISO/IEC 27001:2013).

Kanade, T., Kittler, J., Kleinberg, J. M., Mattern, F., Mitchell, J. C., Nierstrasz, O.,. . . Zuccherato, R. J. (Eds.). (2004). *Selected Areas in Cryptography. Lecture Notes in Computer Science*. Berlin, Heidelberg: Springer Berlin Heidelberg.

Karame, G., & Androulaki, E. (2016). *Bitcoin and blockchain security. Artech House information security and privacy series*. Norwood, MA: Artech House.

Kiayias, A., Russel, A., Bernardo, D., & Oliynykov, R. (2017). Ouroboros: A Provably Secure Proof-of-Stake Blockchain Protocol. In J. Katz & H. Shacham (Eds.), *Lecture Notes in Computer Science: Vol. 10401. Advances in Cryptology - CRYPTO 2017: 37th Annual International Cryptology Conference, Santa Barbara, CA, USA, August 20-24, 2017 : proceedings* (pp. 357–388). Cham: Springer.

Kirk, J., & Miller, M. L. (2005). *Reliability and validity in qualitative research* ([Nachdr.]). *Sage university paper: Vol. 1.* Newbury Park, Calif.: Sage.

Kissel, R. (2013). *Glossary of key information security terms*: National Institute of Standards and Technology.

Lai, R., & LEE Kuo Chuen, D. (2018). Blockchain – From Public to Private. In *Handbook of Blockchain, Digital Finance, and Inclusion, Volume 2* (pp. 145–177). Elsevier. https://doi.org/10.1016/B978-0-12-812282-2.00007-3

Li, X., Jiang, P., Chen, T., Luo, X., & Wen, Q. (2017). A survey on the security of blockchain systems. *Future Generation Computer Systems.* Advance online publication. https://doi.org/10.1016/j.future.2017.08.020

Liamputtong, P., & Ezzy, D. (2006). *Qualitative research methods* (2nd ed.). Oxford: Oxford University Press.

Litecoin Foundation. (2018). Block hashing algorithm. Retrieved from https://litecoin.info/index.php/Block_hashing_algorithm

Loshin, D. (2011). *The practitioner's guide to data quality improvement. The MK / OMG Press.* Amsterdam: Morgan Kaufmann/Elsevier.

Marschan-Piekkari, R. (Ed.). (2004). *Handbook of qualitative research methods for international business.* Cheltenham: Elgar.

Martinsson, J., Dumitrescu, D., & Riedel, K. (2016). Recruiting an Online Panel from another Online Survey: Consequences of Framing and Placement of the Recruitment Question. *International Journal of Public Opinion Research*, *53*, edw005. https://doi.org/10.1093/ijpor/edw005

Mayring, P. (2000). Qualitative Content Analysis. *Forum: Qualitative Social Research*, *1*(2).

Mazieres, D. (2016). The Stellar Consensus Protocol: A Federated Model for Internet-level Consensus. Retrieved from https://www.stellar.org/papers/stellar-consensus-protocol.pdfhttps://www.stellar.org/papers/stellar-consensus-protocol.pdf

Merna, T., & Al-Thani, F. F. (2008). *Corporate risk management* (2nd ed.). Chichester, England, Hoboken, NJ: Wiley.

Miles, M. B., Huberman, A. M., & Saldaña, J. (2014). *Qualitative data analysis: A methods sourcebook* (Edition 3). Los Angeles, London, New Delhi, Singapore, Washington DC: Sage.

Nakamoto, S. (2008). *Bitcoin: A Peer-to-Peer Electronic Cash System*. Retrieved from https://bitcoin.org/bitcoin.pdf

National Institute of Standards and Technology. (2013). *Digital Signature Standard (DSS)*: National Institute of Standards and Technology.

National Institute of Standards and Technology. (2018). *Framework for Improving Critical Infrastructure Cybersecurity*.

Neuendorf, K. A. (2010). *The content analysis guidebook* (9. [print.]). Thousand Oaks: Sage Publ.

Neuron. (2018). List of cryptocurrency exchange hacks. Retrieved from https://rados.io/list-of-documented-exchange-hacks/#fnref1

Perry, C., Riege, A., & Brown, L. (1999). Realism's role among scientific paradigms in marketing research (1999). *Rish Marketing Review*, *12*(2), 16–23.

Popov, S. (2017). The Tangle. Retrieved from https://iotatoken.com/IOTA_Whitepaper.pdf

Raval, S. (2016). *Decentralized applications: Harnessing Bitcoin's Blockchain technology* (First edition). Sebastopol, CA: O'Reilly Media.

Risius, M., & Spohrer, K. (2017). A Blockchain Research Framework. *Business & Information Systems Engineering*, *59*(6), 385–409. https://doi.org/10.1007/s12599-017-0506-0

Schneider, F. B. (1990). Implementing fault-tolerant services using the state machine approach: A tutorial. *ACM Computing Surveys*, *22*(4), 299–319. https://doi.org/10.1145/98163.98167

Schwartz, D., Youngs, N., & Britto, A. (2014). The Ripple Protocol Consensus Algorithm. Retrieved from https://ripple.com/files/ripple_consensus_whitepaper.pdf

Sue, V. M., & Ritter, L. A. (2007). *Conducting online surveys*. Los Angeles: Sage Publications.

Swan, M. (2015). *Blockchain: Blueprint for a new economy* (1. ed.). *Safari Tech Books Online*. Beijing: O'Reilly.

Szabo, N. (1997). Formalizing and Securing Relationships on Public Networks. *First Monday, 2*(9). https://doi.org/10.5210/fm.v2i9.548

Tanenbaum, A. S., & van Steen, M. (2016). *Distributed systems: Principles and paradigms* (Second edition, adjusted for digital publishing). Leiden: Maarten van Steen.

Thompson, P. (2018, January 1). Bitcoin Adoption by Businesses in 2017. *CoinTelegraph*. Retrieved from https://cointelegraph.com/news/bitcoin-adoption-by-businesses-in-2017

Vacca, J. R. (Ed.). (2017). *Computer and information security handbook* (Third edition). Cambridge, MA: Morgan Kaufmann.

Weber, I., Gramoli, V., Ponomarev, A., Staples, M., Holz, R., Tran, A. B., & Rimba, P. (2017). On Availability for Blockchain-Based Systems. In *2017 IEEE 36th Symposium on Reliable Distributed Systems (SRDS)* (pp. 64–73). IEEE. https://doi.org/10.1109/SRDS.2017.15

Weller, R. (2007). *Introduction to the new mainframe: Security* (1st ed.). *IBM redbooks*: IBM International Technical Support Organization.

Zikmund, W. G. (2009). *Business research methods* (8. ed.). Mason, Ohio: Thomson/South-Western.

Appendix

1 Category Definitions

ID	Title	Definition	Coding Unit
D1	Consensus Attack (51% Attack)	A threat where an individual or an organization controls the majority of the mining power	Clear meaning component (seme) in the text
D2	Low Quality Smart Contract Code	Code on a blockchain that contains errors or has no error handling implemented is a threat to data integrity	Clear meaning component (seme) in the text
D4	Alternative Chain	A situation occurs where the blockchain forks itself, without any political background	Clear meaning component (seme) in the text
D5	Misuse of Private Key	Somebody controls a private key he is not the real owner of	Clear meaning component (seme) in the text
D6	Incorrect Data Input	Wrong or incorrect data is stored on the blockchain which can mislead users	Clear meaning component (seme) in the text
D8	A blockchain contains historical data	A blockchain contains historical data and therefor threatens the actuality of the data	Clear meaning component (seme) in the text
D9	Node is malicious / out of sync	A node where a client connects to is not properly synchronized to the network or the node acts malicious in another way	Clear meaning component (seme) in the text
D11	Data on the blockchain cannot be deleted	Data stored on the blockchain is permanent and cannot be removed as the blockchain network exists	Clear meaning component (seme) in the text
D13	No Central Authority	A blockchain is a decentralized system and therefor has no central authority that controls the data flow or transactions	Clear meaning component (seme) in the text
D14	Trust in Protocol Developers	The developers of the blockchain protocol code has to be trusted that they don't misuse the power to their advantage	Clear meaning component (seme) in the text
D15	Trust in Third Parties	Users have to trust third parties that they don't abuse their power to their advantage	Clear meaning component (seme) in the text

A

2 Survey

The starting page of the survey provides information about who conducts the survey, the purpose of the survey, how the data is handled and whom to contact in case of any questions.

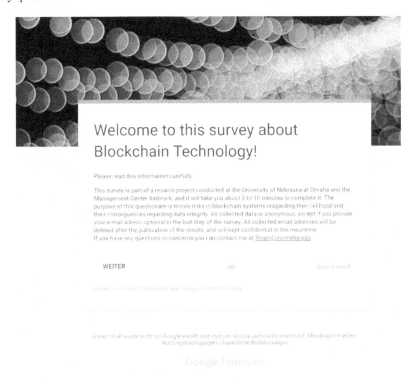

The next section of the survey collects the demographic data.

Welcome to this survey about
Blockchain Technology!

* Erforderlich

Demographics

Please provide your demographic information. This data is only used for survey participant statistics.

What is your age? *

What is your highest degree you received? *

What is your current occupation? *

ZURÜCK   WEITER

The next section will determine the likelihood of the identified risks. This section only contains 9 out of 11 eleven risks. Because 2 risks are not rated among their likelihood.

Likelihood of Scenarios

Please rate the following scenarios how likley do you think they will occur when using a large scale public blockchain system (e.g. Bitcoin, Ethereum, …)

An attacker performs a consensus attack (51% attack) *

	1	2	3	4	5	6	7	8	9	10	
Very Rare	○	○	○	○	○	○	○	○	○	○	Almost Certain

Bad quality code (e.g. in a smart contract) produces an invalid state on the blockchain *

	1	2	3	4	5	6	7	8	9	10	
Very Rare	○	○	○	○	○	○	○	○	○	○	Almost Certain

There is an inadvertent fork of the blockchain *

	1	2	3	4	5	6	7	8	9	10	
Very Rare	○	○	○	○	○	○	○	○	○	○	Almost Certain

Somebody is able to abuse a private key *

	1	2	3	4	5	6	7	8	9	10	
Very Rare	○	○	○	○	○	○	○	○	○	○	Almost Certain

Somebody publishes wrong data on a blockchain *

	1	2	3	4	5	6	7	8	9	10	
Very Rare	○	○	○	○	○	○	○	○	○	○	Almost Certain

The node, which you are connected to is not synchronized to the network, or acts malicious *

	1	2	3	4	5	6	7	8	9	10	
Very Rare	○	○	○	○	○	○	○	○	○	○	Almost Certain

The missing of a central authority will lead to a malfunction of the blockchain *

	1	2	3	4	5	6	7	8	9	10	
Very Rare	○	○	○	○	○	○	○	○	○	○	Almost Certain

The developers of the blockchain protocol abuses their power *

	1	2	3	4	5	6	7	8	9	10	
Very Rare	○	○	○	○	○	○	○	○	○	○	Almost Certain

A trusted third party (e.g. a cryptocurrency exchange) abuses their power *

	1	2	3	4	5	6	7	8	9	10	
Very Rare	○	○	○	○	○	○	○	○	○	○	Almost Certain

D

The following section informs the user about the intention of the following questions

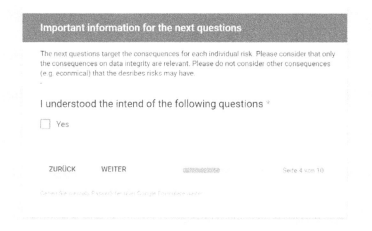

The following section rates the risks among their consequences on data integrity. All eleven risks are rated in this section.

Consequences to data integrity of Scenarios

Please rate the following scenarios how grave do you think the consequences regarding data integrity will be when using a large scale public blockchain system (e.g. Bitcoin, Ethereum, ...).

An attacker performs a consensus attack (51% attack) *

 1 2 3 4 5 6 7 8 9 10

Negligible ○ ○ ○ ○ ○ ○ ○ ○ ○ Catastrophic

Bad quality code (e.g. in a smart contract) produces an invalid state on the blockchain *

 1 2 3 4 5 6 7 8 9 10

Negligible ○ ○ ○ ○ ○ ○ ○ ○ ○ Catastrophic

There is an inadvertent fork of the blockchain *

 1 2 3 4 5 6 7 8 9 10

Negligible ○ ○ ○ ○ ○ ○ ○ ○ ○ Catastrophic

Somebody is able to abuse a private key *

 1 2 3 4 5 6 7 8 9 10

Negligible ○ ○ ○ ○ ○ ○ ○ ○ ○ Catastrophic

Somebody publishes wrong data on a blockchain *

 1 2 3 4 5 6 7 8 9 10

Negligible ○ ○ ○ ○ ○ ○ ○ ○ ○ Catastrophic

A blockchain contains historical data and therefore could deliver outdated information *

 1 2 3 4 5 6 7 8 9 10

Negligible ○ ○ ○ ○ ○ ○ ○ ○ ○ Catastrophic

The node, which you are connected to is not synchronized to the network, or acts malicious *

 1 2 3 4 5 6 7 8 9 10

Negligible ○ ○ ○ ○ ○ ○ ○ ○ ○ Catastrophic

There is critical or confidential data on the blockchain that can not be revoked *

 1 2 3 4 5 6 7 8 9 10

Negligible ○ ○ ○ ○ ○ ○ ○ ○ ○ Catastrophic

The missing of a central authority will lead to a malfunction of the blockchain *

 1 2 3 4 5 6 7 8 9 10

Negligible ○ ○ ○ ○ ○ ○ ○ ○ ○ Catastrophic

The developers of the blockchain protocol abuses their power *

 1 2 3 4 5 6 7 8 9 10

Negligible ○ ○ ○ ○ ○ ○ ○ ○ ○ Catastrophic

A trusted third party (e.g. a cryptocurrency exchange) abuses their power *

 1 2 3 4 5 6 7 8 9 10

Negligible ○ ○ ○ ○ ○ ○ ○ ○ ○ Catastrophic

F

The following sections collect data for communicating the results and payment information for the winner.

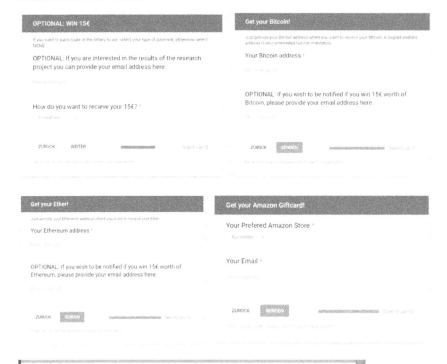

Welcome to this survey about Blockchain Technology!

Your answers have been sent. Thanks for your time and all the best for the lottery if you decided to participate.

3 Code for Visualizations

This Chapter contains the code used to create the visualizations. The code can be copied into an R Markdown file and run. If recreating the graphs, make sure all necessary libraries are installed previously.

```
#Setup
#Used Sources & Information for Chart Creation:
#http://www.sthda.com/english/wiki/ggplot2-essentials
#https://www.r-graph-gallery.com/128-ring-or-donut-plot/
#https://www.r-graph-gallery.com/305-basic-circle-packing-with-one-level/
#http://r-statistics.co/Top50-Ggplot2-Visualizations-MasterList-R-
Code.html

knitr::opts_chunk$set(echo =TRUE)
library("ggplot2")
library("reshape2")
library("data.table")
##
## Attaching package: 'data.table'
## The following objects are masked from 'package:reshape2':
##
##      dcast, melt
library("ggrepel")
library("matrixStats")
library("plyr")
##
## Attaching package: 'plyr'
## The following object is masked from 'package:matrixStats':
##
##      count
library("packcircles")
library("gplots")
##
## Attaching package: 'gplots'
## The following object is masked from 'package:stats':
##
##      lowess
library("ggalt")
#Read Data
dat =read.csv("data2.csv", sep=";", header=TRUE)
demo =read.csv("demographic.csv", sep=";", header=TRUE)
#Degree Viszualitaion
frequ <-count(demo$Degree)
edu <-as.list(levels(frequ[,1]))

dist <-data.frame(Degree=frequ$x, Frequency=frequ$freq)

dist$fraction =dist$Frequency /sum(dist$Frequency)
dist =dist[order(-dist$fraction),]
```

```
dist$Degree <-ordered(dist$Degree, levels =c("Masters degree","Bachelors de-
gree", "Doctorate degree (Ph.D. or Ed.D.)", "Associate degree", "High school
diploma or the equivalent (GED)"))

dist$ymax =cumsum(dist$fraction)
dist$ymin =c(0, head(dist$ymax, n=-1))
ggplot(dist, aes(fill=dist$Degree, ymax=dist$ymax, ymin=dist$ymin, xmax=4,
xmin=3)) +
geom_rect() +
coord_polar(theta="y") +
xlim(c(1, 4)) +
theme(panel.grid=element_blank()) +
labs(title="Highest degree of survey participants n=41") +
theme(panel.grid.major.x =element_blank()) +
theme(axis.ticks =element_blank()) +
theme(panel.background =element_blank()) +
theme(panel.grid.minor =element_blank()) +
theme(plot.title =element_text(hjust =0.5)) +
labs(fill='Degree') +
scale_fill_manual(values=c("#05668D",                         "#028090",
"#00A896","#02C39A","#F3E5B2")) +
geom_label(aes(label=paste(dist$Frequency),x=3.5,y=(ymin+ymax)/2),in-
herit.aes =TRUE, show.legend =FALSE) +
theme(axis.title=element_blank()) +
theme(axis.text=element_blank())
```

```
#Age Distribution Vizualization
medianAge <-median(demo$Age)
ggplot(data=demo, aes(demo$Age)) +
geom_histogram(aes(y =..count..),
col="#03324C",
fill="#028090",
alpha = .2) +
geom_density(col="#02C39A", fill="#02C39A", alpha =0.2, aes(y = ..density..
*40)) +
labs(title="Distribution of Age for Survey Participants n=41") +
labs(x="Age", y="Count") +
theme(panel.background =element_blank()) +
theme(plot.title =element_text(hjust =0.5)) +
geom_vline(aes(xintercept =median(demo$Age)),col='red',size=2) +
annotate("text", x=medianAge +4, y=6, label=paste("Median Age =", medianAge,
sep=" ")) +
theme(panel.grid.major.y =element_line(size=0.5, colour="grey93", line-
type="solid")) +
scale_y_continuous(breaks=seq(0,6,1)) +
scale_x_continuous(breaks=seq(18,52,4)) +
scale_y_continuous(sec.axis =sec_axis(~./40, name="Density"))
## Scale for 'y' is already present. Adding another scale for 'y', which
## will replace the existing scale.
## `stat_bin()` using `bins = 30`. Pick better value with `binwidth`.
```

J

```
#Occupation Vizualization
occu <-count(demo$Standardized)
x_limits <-c(1.07, NA)
occu$x          <-ordered(occu$x,          levels=c("Consultant","Business
Owner","Other","IT-Specialist","Student", "Software Developer"))
ggplot(occu, aes(x=1, y=freq, label=paste(x," [",freq,"]",sep=" "))) +
geom_bar(stat="identity",width =0.1,aes(fill=x)) +
scale_fill_manual(val-
ues=c("#E3E5B2","#02C39A","#00A896","#028090","#05668D","#03324C")) +
geom_label_repel(aes(colour=x),show.legend =FALSE,size=4, position =posi-
tion_stack(vjust  =0.5),   xlim=x_limits,   force=10,arrow  =arrow(length
=unit(0.03, "npc"), type ="closed", ends ="first")) +
scale_colour_manual(values=c("#E3E5B2","#02C39A","#00A896","#028090","#056
68D","#03324C")) +
theme(panel.grid.major.x =element_blank()) +
theme(axis.title.x=element_blank())+
theme(axis.text.x=element_blank())+
theme(panel.grid.major.y  =element_line(size=0.5,  colour="grey93",  line-
type="solid")) +
theme(legend.position="none") +
theme(axis.ticks =element_blank()) +
theme(panel.background =element_blank()) +
theme(panel.grid.minor =element_blank()) +
theme(plot.title =element_text(hjust =0.5)) +
ggtitle("Occupations of Participants n=41") +
ylab ("Participant Count") +
#coord_flip() +
scale_x_continuous(limits=c(0.85, 1.15)) +
scale_y_continuous(limits=c(0, 45),breaks=seq(0,45,5)) +
guides(fill=guide_legend(title="Occupation"))
```

```r
#Likelihood Vizualization
likelihood =dat[c(2:12)]
ggplot(data =melt(likelihood), aes(x=variable, y=value)) +
geom_boxplot(aes(fill=variable), outlier.shape =NA) +
theme(panel.grid.major.x =element_blank()) +
theme(panel.grid.major.y =element_line(size=0.5,  colour="grey93",  line-
type="solid")) +
theme(legend.position="none") +
theme(axis.ticks =element_blank()) +
theme(panel.background =element_blank()) +
theme(panel.grid.minor =element_blank()) +
theme(plot.title =element_text(hjust =0.5)) +
ggtitle("Likelihood of Risk Occurance n=41") +
xlab("Risk ID") +
ylab ("Probability of Occurrence") +
scale_y_continuous(limits=c(0.9, 10),breaks=seq(1,10,1))
## No id variables; using all as measure variables

#Consequences Vizualization
consequences =dat[c(13:23)]
ggplot(data =melt(consequences), aes(x=variable, y=value)) +
geom_boxplot(aes(fill=variable), outlier.shape =NA) +
theme(panel.grid.major.x =element_blank()) +
theme(panel.grid.major.y =element_line(size=0.5,  colour="grey93",  line-
type="solid")) +
theme(legend.position="none") +
theme(axis.ticks =element_blank()) +
theme(panel.background =element_blank()) +
theme(panel.grid.minor =element_blank()) +
theme(plot.title =element_text(hjust =0.5)) +
ggtitle("Consequences for Data Integrity of potential Risks n=41") +
xlab("Risk ID") +
ylab ("Severity of Consequences") +
scale_y_continuous(limits=c(0.9, 10),breaks=seq(1,10,1))
## No id variables; using all as measure variables
```

```
#Risk Matrix
likelihood <-data.matrix(likelihood, rownames.force =NA)
like <-colMedians(likelihood)
like <-as.list(like)

consequences <-data.matrix(consequences, rownames.force =NA)
cons <-colMedians(consequences)
cons <-as.list(cons)

ids<-c("D1","D2","D4","D5","D6","D8", "D9", "D11", "D13", "D14", "D15")
rating      <-do.call(rbind,   Map(data.frame,   Likelihood=like,   Conse-
quences=cons))
rating$score <-rowSums(rating)
rating$category <- ""


rating <-within(rating, {
  category[score <4] <- "Very Low"
  category[score <8&score >=4] <- "Low"
  category[score <12&score >=8] <- "Medium"
  category[score <=16&score >=12] <- "High"
  category[score >16] <- "Very High"
  category[is.na(score)] <- ""
})

rating$category <-as.factor(rating$category)
row.names(rating)    <-c("D1","D2","D4","D5","D6","D8","D9","D11",    "D13",
"D14", "D15")
high <-rating[ which(rating$category=='High'), ]
medium <-rating[ which(rating$category=='Medium'), ]
low <-rating[ which(rating$category=='Low'), ]

rating <-rating[order(rating$score),]
ggplot(rating, aes(x=rating$Likelihood, y=rating$Consequences, colour = rat-
ing$score)) +
geom_point(size=6, alpha=0.6, position=position_jitter(h=0.1, w=0.1)) +
theme(panel.grid.major.x  =element_line(size=0.5,  colour="grey93",  line-
type="solid")) +
theme(panel.grid.major.y  =element_line(size=0.5,  colour="grey93",  line-
type="solid")) +
theme(axis.ticks =element_blank()) +
theme(panel.background =element_blank()) +
theme(panel.grid.minor =element_blank()) +
theme(plot.title =element_text(hjust =0.5)) +
ggtitle("Risk Matrix") +
labs(colour='Risk Score') +
geom_text_repel(aes(label=row.names(rating)),hjust=0.5,          vjust=2.2,
show.legend =FALSE) +
scale_y_continuous(limits=c(0.89,10.11),breaks=seq(1,10,1)) +
scale_x_continuous(limits=c(0.5,10.39),breaks=seq(1,10.39,1)) +
xlab("Likelihood of Risk") +
ylab("Consequences for Data Integrity") +
```

M

```
scale_colour_continuous(low="green",      high="red",      limits=c(3.99,16),
breaks=c(4,7,10,13,16)) +
geom_encircle(aes(x=high$Likelihood,      y=high$Consequences),      data=high,
color="red", size=1.1, expand=0.11) +
geom_encircle(aes(x=medium$Likelihood, y=medium$Consequences), data=medium,
color="orange", size=1.1, expand=0.03) +
geom_encircle(aes(x=low$Likelihood,      y=low$Consequences),      data=low,
color="green", size=1.1, expand=-0.03) +
annotate("text", x=8, y=9, label=paste("High Risk")) +
annotate("text", x=2.2, y=8, label=paste("Medium Risk")) +
annotate("text", x=1, y=4.2, label=paste("Low Risk"))
```

4 Consent Sheet

Information sheet.
FOR STUDY PARTICIPANTS

You are invited to participate in a research study. Before you decide on whether to participate, it is important you understand why the research is done and how exactly you will be involved. Please take time to read the following information before you decide whether or not you wish to participate.

Title of study: Data Integrity Risks on Public Blockchain Systems

Study purposes
This study aims to identify risks regarding data integrity in public blockchain systems. This research is part of the master's Thesis of the researcher.

Participants
The study targets expert in the domain of blockchain systems.

Participation Instructions
If you agree to take part in this study, you will be asked to answers several interview. Your answers will be recorded with an appropriate device. You can ask any questions during the interview.

Study Duration
Completing the interview will require approx. 15 minutes of your time.

Do you have to take part in this study?
The participation in this interview is entirely voluntary. You can withdraw from the interview at any time without having to provide a reason. You can also withhold answers to questions asked by the interviewer if you do not feel comfortable answering them.

Reward
You will not be offered a reward for participating in this interview. However, your participation may serve science, and ultimately, help improve the future development and adoption of blockchain systems.

Data Treatment
Neither personal nor private data will be recorded during the study. The data that you will provide will not let anyone identify you as a participant. The collected data will be used in statistical analyses and may be presented to an audience in an aggregated form, and may be published as an open-access dataset for research.

What happens now?
If you would like to participate in the study, please read through the study consent form, ask the study researcher the questions you may have, and sign the consent form. After that, a researcher will begin with the interview.

0

Informed Consent.
TO BE PROVIDED TO STUDY PARTICIPANTS

I understand that my participation in this study will involve me **answering a number of questions.**

I understand that this will in total **require approximately** **16** **minutes** of my time.

I understand that while I answer the questions, the **audio is recorded,** and the interviewer may take any **notes of my behaviour.**

I understand that the recorded data will be **anonymized** and used for research purposes. I agree that my data will be used for scientific purposes and I have no objection that my data is published in scientific publications in a way that does not reveal my identity.

I understand that participation in this study is entirely voluntary and that I can withdraw from the study at any time without giving a reason. I understand that in case I withdraw from the study, all the data that has arisen from my contribution will be removed unless it has already been published.

I understand that I am free to **ask any questions** about the study and to discuss my concerns about the study with the research assistant.

I understand that I can subsequently contact the researcher if I wish to obtain a copy of any publications derived from the research.

I understand that the information provided by me will be held anonymously so that it is impossible to trace this information back to me individually.

I, ... consent to participate in this study conducted by

www.ingramcontent.com/pod-product-compliance
Lightning Source LLC
La Vergne TN
LVHW092341060326
832902LV00008B/758